A CONFIDENT CENTURY

Published for

Stratford-on-Avon Golf Club

in

A Limited Edition of 1,000 copies

Copy Nº **274**

Ludford Docker – Forethought and generosity secured the land at Tiddington Road – 1924

Pat Barrett – generosity and guidance 50's–70's.
'PB' with four of his principle aides. Left to right:
Fred Kitchen. PB. Laurie Dobson. Stan Tyas. Bob Robinson.

Nicky Tarratt –
Champion Golfer 80's–
90's
*Photo: Coventry Evening
Telegraph*

Some Prominent Members
of the Century

A CONFIDENT CENTURY

STRATFORD-ON-AVON

GOLF CLUB

1894 – 1994

John Gee

A Square One Publication

First published in 1994 by
Square One Publications, Saga House
Sansome Place, Worcester WR1 1UA

© Stratford-on-Avon Golf Club 1994

British Library Cataloguing in Publication Data

Gee, John
  A Confident Century: Stratford-on-Avon Golf Club 1894–1994
  I. Title
  796.35206
  ISBN 1-872017-78-9

Typeset by Avon Dataset Ltd, Waterloo Road, Bidford-on-Avon, B50 4JH
Printed by Biddles Ltd, Guildford, England

Contents

Acknowledgements   vii
Introduction   viii
Foreword by Peter Alliss   x
Message from the President (Prologue)   xi
Message from the Captain   xii

1894–1897: Wilmcote
Foundation of the Club   1

1897–1926: Welcombe Fields
The Land   11
Activity Commences at Welcombe   13
Firm Progress by the Club   17
1909–1914: The Five Years Prior to the First World War   23
The First World War 1914–1918   24
The Post War Era   28
Expansion and Improvement of the Club   33
Negotiation and Construction of a New Course at Tiddington
    Road   35
Conversion to Limited Company and Final Days at Welcombe 36

1925–1994: Tiddington Road
Early Days   45
The influence of Sam Ryder   50
Great Golfers at Opening Matches on New Course – George
    Duncan – Abe Mitchell – Ted Ray – Alex Herd and
    Whitcombe brothers   60
Official Opening of the New Course   61
Consolidation at Tiddington Road 1931–1939   80
Second World War 1939–1945   82
Gravel Extraction   82
Royal Air Force at Stratford   83

The Immediate Post War Era 1945–1950   86

Exhibition Match – Henry Cotton at Stratford   87

The Fifties – Progress with Course and Amenities.   90

*The Sixties – The Course Transformed with Extensive Tree
  Planting*   97

*The Seventies – Big Improvements to Course and Premises.
  Increasing Financial Demands*   102

Modern Times – The Eighties and Nineties   109

The Ladies

Message from the Ladies Captain   116

Early Personalities at Welcombe Fields   116

1936 – The Ladies Begin to Make Their Mark   122

Officers, Champions and Course Records   142

Miscellaneous – reflections and records

The Course today   147

Golfing feats   148

'I remember'   155

Profiles   163

Message from Club Chairman (Epilogue)   171

Captains, Presidents and principle trophies   171

Club Champions and Course Records   174

Acknowledgements

I am most grateful to the many people who gave their time, and passed on their recollections of Stratford-on-Avon Golf Club.

My especial thanks go to; Harry Brook, Margaret Chadwick, Peter and Anna Clarke, Laurie Dobson, Anne Layton and Stan Thomas who read the early manuscript, corrected many of my errors and passed wise comment on the content. Anne Layton, again, for all her help with the Ladies Section, Colonel 'Tinker' Jackson for help in persuading Peter Alliss to write the foreword; Dr Robert Bearman and Mairi MacDonald of the Shakespeare Centre, Stratford-upon-Avon, for their help researching their records. Ian Frimston for many hours taking, copying and printing photographs. Ted Evans of Milson, Kidderminster for his recollections and drawing of the Welcombe Course, and both Ted and Letitia for their hospitality when Joan and I visited them. Molly Moore for the loan of her valuable albums and flags; Margaret Chadwick, Ann Gibbs, John Humphreys, Jennifer Miramadi, Violet Simpson and Nancy Thomas for the loan of photographs and newspaper cuttings; Cynthia Walkden for so many photocopies, and my daughter Sue and grandson Peter Chaplin for many hours spent on their word processor.

For profiles of some prominent members and personal recollections of events on the course and in the Clubhouse, I am particularly grateful to Leslie Ball, Pat Brownsdon, Vic Burn, Laurie Dobson, Ted Marson, David Moffatt, Jack Mound, Richard Ollis, Neville Tarratt, Freddie Walker and Violet Simpson, Peter Rodgers for providing some golfing feats and statistics, and last but not least Harry Drury for editing the final manuscript, and Arthur & Babs Ridley for their help in proofreading.

I thank all the above and many others who contributed, and made me so welcome on visits in my quest for information.

Above all I thank Joan for being patient and understanding, for putting up with an untidy office and the clatter of my typewriter, on and off, for the past three years, and for providing a constant flow of coffee.

J.G.

Introduction

In December 1986, during my year as Captain of Stratford-on-Avon Golf Club, my guest speaker at the Annual Dinner was that very distinguished airman, Walker Cup Captain, and author, P B (Laddie) Lucas CBE DSO DFC. During conversation over dinner he asked, "When is your Centenary?" When I told him it would be in 1994, he immediately advised not to leave it too late, if we envisaged writing the Club's history. He had experienced writing such projects at some well known clubs and knew how long it would take.

This seemed an interesting subject and one which appealed to me, so with the approval of the Committee I made a start.

At intervals since then I have attempted to write an accurate history of the first one hundred years of Stratford-on-Avon Golf Club.

In March 1991, however, the project very nearly came to a sudden halt. Returning home from researching records at the Shakespeare Centre in Stratford-upon-Avon, I was involved in a head-on collision. A car being driven far too fast in the opposite direction, braked, locked all four wheels and came straight at me, as I took refuge in the hedge of Charlecote Park. Fortunately the result was nothing more serious than one car written off and mine very badly bent.

Although incomplete, many of the Club minutes, since inception, were available, and these together with newspaper cuttings and journals, unearthed with the help of Dr Robert Bearman and Mairi McDonald at the Shakespeare Centre, and some members, have been the main documentary source of information.

Over and above this I have had the personal recollections of many individuals.

Obviously I cannot claim any personal knowledge of many of the events I have described, and it may well be that in writing about them from records, that I have taken the wrong view.

Also there are many individuals to whom I must have failed to give due credit and who have made significant contributions to the

Stratford-on-Avon Golf Club over many years. This is entirely due to ignorance on my part, and I sincerely trust that they will accept my apologies.

Inevitably there will be criticism as to why 'old so and so' is not mentioned, and why 'such and such' an event has been left out. All I can do is to apologise and say that I have had to rely on what I have been able to dig out, and what has come in, and be thankful that in the end I obtained so much.

I feel very proud and privileged to have been a member of Stratford-on-Avon Golf Club, for the past twenty years, and to have been Captain in 1986 and in writing this history I hope, in some small way, to repay the Club for the many happy times that I have had there.

I have no doubt that in the next hundred years the Club will remain as eminent as it is now and provide much enjoyment for members and visitors alike.

J. G.

Foreword by Peter Alliss

Stratford-on-Avon Golf Club Centenary 1994

Golf has been my life for more than 50 years. During that time much has happened to change the face of the game. Much of it good, some of it, well, I'm not so sure. But one thing is for certain, it is always a very special occasion when a Club celebrates its centenary.

Years ago such a milestone was indeed rare. As the years go by more and more Clubs celebrate the enchanting 100 so perhaps a little of the early glamour has gone, but for any Club celebrating the magic figure things are indeed special.

My earliest recollections of the Stratford Golf Club were more years ago than I care to remember. It was an exhibition match played for the Lord Robert's Work Shops and Forces Help Society. What a fun occasion it was. Indeed, the gallant band usually consisting of Dai Rees and David Thomas competing against Bernard Hunt and yours truly, England v Wales, what fun we had.

I immediately liked the 'feel' at Stratford. It reminded me so much of my early days in golf, the comfortable chairs, the honours boards reflecting those of stature and interest who had gone before, plus so much more. Another special reason for my enjoyment of the Club was my friendship with Colonel 'Tinker' Jackson CBE, a long time friend of my wife's family and a great lover of the game of golf. 'Tinker' has always kept me informed of the 'doings' at Stratford, so, although my visits over the years have been few, I have been kept well up to date with the happenings at the Club.

Congratulations on your centenary, here's to the next 100.

Prologue

*President's Centenary Year
Message*

From the President — Mr Laurie G Dobson.

It is over forty years since I played my first game of golf at Stratford-on-Avon Golf Club. In those seemingly uncomplicated and care-free days, long before the advent of computers, mobile phones etc, and before the days of televised golf, a round of golf could be completed in under three hours. It seemed such a simple game in those halcyon days.

Alas we cannot put the clock back, nor should we perhaps, except to thank and remember all those past and present members who had the foresight, dedication and energy to provide us with a Club which is held in high esteem.

We must now look forward to the next hundred years ensuring that we pass on to our successors in good heart the heritage we now enjoy.

Our thanks go to John Gee who has spent some three years researching the beginnings of the Club and its subsequent development during the past century.

Thanks also to the many members and others who have provided additional information and photographs and to Francis Prentice and the Centenary Committee for organising the celebrations.

I am honoured and privileged to have been elected your President during this Centenary Year and I send my very best wishes to you all.

Laurie Dobson

The Captain's Centenary Year Message.

From the Captain — Mr Clive Walford.

Centenary Year is a very special year for any organisation and Stratford-on-Avon Golf Club is very proud to be celebrating 100 years of golf in 1994.

It is appropriate that in this year we should pay tribute to all those members and staff, past and present, whose enthusiasm, hard work and dedication, have made Stratford-on-Avon Golf Club what it is today.

I hope that in future, members and staff, with these same qualities, will continue to work positively for the development and improvement of the Club.

Thanks are due to Francis Prentice and the Centenary Committee who have worked tirelessly to ensure that 1994 will be a year to remember.

I consider it a great honour to be invited to be Club Captain in this special year.

Clive Walford

A Confident Century –

Stratford-on-Avon Golf Club:

1894–1994

Foundation of the Club

It was in 1894 when Queen Victoria still had seven years to reign, and Lord Roseberry was Prime Minister that Stratford-on-Avon Golf Club was founded.

The Club's first home was at Wilmcote, a small village, where the Bard's father came courting many years ago, as is made clear to travellers on the A3400, by the signpost indicating it is the home of Mary Arden's House. This charming village and the home of Shakespeare's mother is certainly well worth a visit for the sense of history alone. It was here that the Stratford-on-Avon Golf Club was formed in June 1894.

An inaugural meeting was held on 30th June 1894 at the Union Club, Stratford-upon-Avon. Mr Stephen Moore presided, and there were present six gentlemen and three ladies. The meeting had been called for the purpose of adopting rules and making all arrangements in connection with the formation of a Golf Club.

Those present were informed that an agreement had been entered into with Mr Badger, the tenant of Wilmcote Moor Farm, land owned by Mr Brewster Norbury, whereby the Club had liberty to play golf on the farm, with the use of a stable, barn and one room in the cottage, for a rent of £2-10-0 up to Michaelmas 1894 and afterwards at an annual rent of £5-0-0, tenancy being determinable by three months' notice on either side.

It was reported that a nine hole course had been laid out by J Cunningham, professional to the Arden Golf Club, Solihull, on this farm about one mile from Wilmcote Station and four miles from Stratford-upon-Avon. Mr Cunningham had pronounced the ground capable of being made into one of the best links in the neighbourhood.

Stratford-on-Avon Golf Club

On the 30th June 1894

A Preliminary Meeting was held at the Union Club Stratford-on-Avon for the purpose of adopting Rules and making all necessary arrangements in connection with the formation of a Golf Club.

Mr. Stephen Moore presided and there were also present Mrs & Miss Hunt, Miss Barrett, Messrs Buckner, Everard, Park, Lowndes, Drees, W. Norbury.

It was reported that an Agreement had been entered into with Mr Badger the tenant of Welcombe Moor Farm whereby the Club have liberty to play Golf on the farm with the use of a Stable, Barn and one room in the Cottage for £2.10.0 up to Michaelmas 1894 and afterwards at the annual rent of £5 the tenancy being determinable by three months notice on either side.

It was also reported that a Course had been laid out by J. Cunninghame Professional to the Arden Golf Club, Solihull who had pronounced the ground capable of being made into one of the best Links in the neighbourhood.

Minutes of Inaugural Meeting 30th June 1894

2

The Rules of the Warwickshire Golf Club and also those of the Worcestershire Golf Club were read and considered, and a set of Rules based upon these, with certain alterations, were adopted for this Club and ordered to be printed.

A Committee of Management to act until the First Annual General Meeting were elected viz. The Revd R. S. de C Laffan, Mr. B. J. Bucknall, Mr. E. L. Larkin, and Mr. Stephen Moore with Mr. C.E. Martin as Hony. Treasurer and Mr. W. Norbury as Hony Secretary

The thanks of the Meeting were given to Mr. Bucknall for having originated the idea of a Golf Club for Stratford-on-Avon.

The rules of the Warwickshire and the Worcester Golf Club were read out and considered, and a set of rules based on these with certain alterations was adopted. A Committee of Management to act until the first Annual General Meeting was elected, with Mr W Norbury as Hon Secretary and Mr C B Martin as Hon Treasurer. The thanks of the meeting were given to Mr B J Bucknall for having originated the idea of a Golf Club for Stratford-upon-Avon.

Apart from the formation of the Stratford-on-Avon Club, the year 1894 was an important year in the history of golf. In that year the British Open Golf Championship was played in England for the first time. It was held at Sandwich and was won by J H Taylor. He was the first English winner – the first of sixteen victories by the triumvirate of J H Taylor, Harry Vardon and James Braid. The same J H Taylor, many years later, planned the new course at Tiddington Road – Stratford-on-Avon Golf Club's third course.

The year 1894 also saw the foundation of the United States Golf Association.

So the year in which the Stratford-on-Avon Club was founded was indeed an important year in golfing history.

Golf Starts

Play began straight away at Wilmcote and before long the layout of the course was increased to 18 holes.

On 2nd November 1894, the Stratford-upon-Avon Herald contained a report headed 'Stratford-on-Avon Golf Club established'. It read:

'We are pleased to learn that the Stratford-on-Avon Golf Club has been established. The royal and ancient game has obtained a firm hold throughout the country so that few places of any importance are without golf links. Wilmcote Moor, being within easy reach by road from Stratford, and within a mile from the Great Western Railway Station at Wilmcote has been chosen as the most suitable site for the links. The course was originally laid out by James Cunningham of Solihull, a well known professional player, and when the 'greens' (which are being taken in hand) have been put into good playing order, the Club, already numbering upwards of fifty members will have one of the best golf links in the midland counties. The "opening" Club competition has just been held. Mr G C Tree securing first place amongst the gentlemen and Miss Agnes Crawford the like honour amongst the ladies.'

On 30th November 1894 the following further report appeared in the Stratford-upon-Avon Herald:

On Saturday last on the links at Wilmcote, the "first" Club competition was held, when Mr W F Hutchings proved the winner with a score of 73 less 10 = 63. There were fourteen competitors. On Wednesday last, over the Ladies' Course, Miss Gwendoline Packe was the winner of the Ladies' Medal with a score of 60 less 8 = 52. There were ten competitors for this event. The recent rains have rendered the course somewhat heavy going and it has not been possible at present to get the greens into anything like condition. A new nine hole course is being laid out, and it is expected that this will be ready for play before Christmas.'

The difference between the 'Opening' and 'First' competitions leaves one puzzled. However the scoring was quite remarkable considering the heavy going and the poor greens. How many holes were the competitions played over?

First Annual General Meeting

The first Annual General Meeting of the Club was held on 4th April 1895 at the Union Club and was attended by 13 gentlemen and three ladies. It was reported that the tenant of the farm, Mr Badger, had intimated his intention to plough the further field, which would preclude golf being played there, or to require more rent.

A discussion took place on the advisability of having a nine hole course against the existing 18 holes, as there was doubt that the funds of the Club would stand the making and keeping in order of 18 putting greens. This matter was left for a special committee appointed to deal with it after conferring with the Committee of Management. The result was a decision to keep 18 holes but to apply any money to be spent on putting greens to the original nine hole course in priority to those on the further nine holes.

The financial position showed a balance in hand of £12-6-6.

An entrance fee for new members was introduced equal to one years' subscription, with the exception of family of existing members.

Twelve months later at the second AGM held on 14th April 1896 Mr G F Kendall was elected the first Captain of the Club. Mr W Norbury, Hon Secretary since the formation of the Club relinquished office and handed over to Mr G C Lowndes, who was to remain Hon Secretary for 23 years.

Rules were again discussed and the rules of the Bromsgrove Golf Club were adopted in place of those drawn up at the inaugural meeting.

The financial position of the Club was reported as satisfactory, the accounts showing a balance of £5-6-9, rather less than 1894 but work had had to be done on the links which had entailed some extra expenditure.

Some golf clubs were unable to play during the summer months, in consequence of their links being laid down for grass. Rule seven was amended to allow members of such clubs to join Stratford-on-Avon. Thus members residing beyond a radius of seven miles of Stratford-upon-Avon could be admitted on payment of Gentlemen 10/6 and Ladies 5/-.

The Wilmcote Links

Regrettably a detailed description of the course at Wilmcote has not been found but an article in the Birmingham Gazette of 7th May 1896 entitled 'On the Links' contained the following comment:

'The links are fairly sportive in character, the hazards consisting of hedges, roadways, a pond, and an old pit. Several of the greens are partly surrounded by bushes, entailing great care and judgement in approaching. So far the Club is not particularly strong in playing members, but time will remedy this defect. Golf, as many of us know to our cost, is not learned in a day; no, nor a year. We know people who have been playing for a good many years, and yet they are not golfers.'

In June 1896 Mr J. Burns, golf professional, was engaged by the

Committee for a short period to improve the Wilmcote links and to coach the members. Mr Burns, a plasterer by trade, had won the Open Championship in 1888 as an 'artisan' golfer.

A New Location

The increasing popularity of the game coupled with the inaccessibility of the course at Wilmcote brought about the search for suitable land nearer the town.

On 17th December 1896 an Extraordinary Meeting of the Club was held at the Memorial Lecture Room to consider a report of the Committee as to a new links. Mr G F Kendall, Captain, presided and in addition to Mr Lowndes, Hon Sec, there were 12 Gentlemen and six ladies present.

The report of the Committee stated that they had received notice from Mr Badger to quit Wilmcote Moor Farm next Lady Day. Mr Fordham Flower had very kindly offered the use of two of his fields, provided the Club could take from Mr Wynne of Welcombe Farm, another field known as the Dingles. This field containing thirty six acres had been secured at a rent of £10 per year fom Michaelmas last, and a course of nine holes had been laid out by a professional player. The putting greens were already formed and it was expected that the new links would very shortly be in sufficient order to begin play. The cost of preparing the links would come to about £18. It was anticipated that by opening links close to the town there would be a considerable accession of members, but the number would depend very largely upon whether a pavilion was provided, and a fund might be raised for this purpose, by way of Certificates of £1-00 each, to be secured upon the building and the rest of the property of the Club, and to bear a small interest. A certain number to be drawn for and paid off each year, after the first year, as the Income and Expenditure account may allow.

A condition of taking the field from Mr Wynne was that a responsible man be engaged by the Club who should have control of the caddies. It was also stated that Mr Wynne had made a stringent condition that no dogs be allowed on the links on any pretext.

The Committee had engaged a greenkeeper, Mr H Fitzjohn, who

7

Financial Statement from 1st April 1896 to 31 March 1897

To Balance in hand from last year 5 6 9

" Subscriptions by:
18 Members at 21/. 18 18
25 ditto at 10/6 .... 13 2 6
2 ditto at 5/. .... 10 .... 32 10 6

" Subscriptions by 1897 only
3 New Members at 40/. 6
5 ditto at 20/. 5
2 Visitors .... 10 6 .... 11 10 6

" Donation from Mr Stevenson 1 1

" Paid in by Members in advance for 1897 -
7 Members at 40/ 14
5 ditto 7/. 5 19

" Balance due to Hon. Treasurer 9 17 10

£79 4 7

Howard
Hon Sec

G. F. Kendall
Captain

James Stevenson
Hon Auditor

Financial Statement year ending 31st March 1897

8

Submitted to the Annual Meeting   April 1897

	At Wilmcote				Forward.	36	4	2
✓	By Badger Rent &c	5		✓	By G. W. Ry. Truck land	12		
✓	" Heads Wages	11	1	✓	" Ashburn — Morris	7		
✓	" Jack Burns Pro	3	11½	✓	" Little Meeting	1	2	
✓	" Her Badger Wages	3	7	6	✓	" Ins & Plant Centre	10	6
✓	" Richard 12 Staid	1	4	✓	" Seckman adverts	6	1	
✓	" Cliffs for Boys Badge	7	3	✓	" Receipt s	1	12	6
✓	" Printing &c	1	4	3	✓	" Fees a/c	17	2	
✓	" Repairs	8	9	✓	" Sundries	1	5	
✓	" Room for Meeting	5		✓	" Cheque book & Stamps	10	5	
✓	" One load sand	5		✓	" Rooms for Meetings	13		
✓	" B. Slag	4	6	✓	" 14 Fit Colm Jan 40/	3	5	
✓	" Oil Sundries	2	7	✓	" ditto 13 Instructors 15/	9	15	
✓	" Coal	1	6	✓	" Ashburn 3 Instructors	8	9	
✓	" Williams for tools	2	12	6	✓	" Repairs 3 Instructors	3	6
		29	17	10	✓	" Kennard for test	11	8
	At Welcombe			✓	" Ditto ladder nails	2	3	6
✓	By Meridon Pro:	16		✓	" Headlands Printing	1		
✓	" Gommery Smith	5	1	8	✓	" Boydon Circulars	6	
✓	" Neale Rolling	9						
						£79	6	7

Carried forward — 36 4 2

Eric Stevenson
Hon: Auditor

C. Lonsdale
Treasurer

G. F. Kendall
Captain

9

was also highly recommended as a coach and club repairer. He had arrived in the town and was lodging at No 49 Great William Street.

Of course it would be necessary to increase subscriptions. A long discussion took place and after several amendments had been proposed the subscriptions were fixed at the following figures, instead of those recommended by the Committee: Gentlemen £2-00, Ladies £1-00.

So three years after its formation the Club moved to Welcombe Fields, and in 1897 the nine hole course was opened close to the Warwick Road.

The expenses of this move are interesting as will be seen from the Balance Sheet for the year ending 31st March 1897.

Welcombe Fields 1897–1926

The Land

In 1896, shortly before the Golf Club moved from Wilmcote to Welcombe Fields, a new member joined the Club, by the name of Trevelyan. Sir George Otto Trevelyan Bart, who was to figure very prominently in the affairs of the Club over the next twenty two years.

At the AGM held on 6th May 1897 Sir George was elected President of the Club and at the same meeting Mr G F Kendall was re-elected Captain.

According to the Stratford Herald of 18th December 1896 which reported the special meeting of the Club held on 17th December, it was Mr Fordham Flower who had offered the Club the use of two fields. However further research indicates that it was probably Mr Archibald Dennis Flower.

A short history of the ownership of the Welcombe land up to that date is therefore appropriate.

In 1815, the Earl of Coventry's estate in Snitterfield was bought by Robert Phillips, a textile magnate from Manchester. Mark, his son, born in 1800, added to this estate in 1844, following the death of his father, by buying the neighbouring Welcombe.

The existing Elizabethan Manor House, which had been converted into a Gothic Mansion, was pulled down. The site remained vacant until 1866, when the foundation stone of the new hall was laid. Four years later Mark Phillips was at last able to move into his new home, although it was not finally completed until after his death in 1874. Mark, a bachelor, was succeeded by his brother Robert Needham Phillips.

It was Robert who had the famous obelisk erected at Snitterfield, to commemorate his father and brother. Robert married and had a daughter Caroline, who later married Sir George Trevelyan in 1869. Caroline inherited the Welcombe estate from her father, when he died in 1890, just four years before the founding of the Stratford-on-Avon Golf Club.

So by 1897 when the Golf Club moved to Welcombe Fields, Sir George and Lady Trevelyan were the landowners; Sir George was the Club President and Messrs Flower and Wynne were their tenants. The Club, as it were, became sub-tenants to the Trevelyans.

As a result of a generous offer by Mr Flower the Club had the use of his two fields, free of charge, and so the only rent the Club paid was to Mr Wynne, £10-00 per annum for the use of the Dingles.

Now was it Archibald Dennis Flower (1865–1950) or Fordham Flower (1904–1966) who made this generous offer? It has also been suggested that it was Archibald's father – but research shows that he was Edgar Flower (1833–1903), who was elected a Vice President of the Club in 1899. It appears thus to have been Archibald, but no matter, the Club was very indebted to Mr Flower for his generosity.

So it was that Stratford-on-Avon Golf Club started on the construction of its second course in the space of three years. The land to be used was that lying to the west of the long driveway, leading from the Warwick Road to Welcombe Lodge, now the Welcombe Hotel.

William Shakespeare and the Royal and Ancient Game

Inevitably, over the years, there has been conjecture at Stratford-upon-Avon as to whether there was any connection between Shakespeare and golf. When Welcombe Fields was chosen as the site for the new course this speculation was very topical, as the land had had very close associations with Shakespeare in the distant past.

This prompted the following comments which appeared in the Stratford-upon-Avon Herald on 19th March 1987:

'So far from there being difficulty to establish a connection the fact is that Shakespeare's works abound in the most direct and explicit references to the pastime in question. Thus we find in "Much Ado about Nothing" an unmistakable allusion to a characteristic St Andrews gesture in the words "I know you by the waggling of

12

your head"; whilst in "Titus Andronicus" we encounter the pertinent query, "What subtle hole is this?" In "Richard III", again, we meet the line "Put in their hands the bruising irons of wrath", and in "Henry VI (Part 1)" the statement "I'll call for clubs". Falstaff's ruling passion was evidently golf, for we know that on his death bed he "babbled of green fields"; and there was certainly a course on Prospero's Island, else why the question, "Why hath the Queen summoned me hither to this short grassed green?" There are we believe some commentators who prefer the reading, "To tee or not to tee, that is the question". But apart from this disputed passage we find in "Hamlet" a reference to the fault of "Slicking too short".

Many other references might be given, but the foregoing are surely enough to prove that Shakespeare had an intimate knowledge of the game.'

The Course at Welcombe Fields

The links situated between the Warwick Road and the Clopton Tower, formed a sporting nine-hole course, commanding superb views of the surrounding country. The hazards were natural, and included the 'Dingles', believed to be ancient entrenchments made during the conflicts between the Britons and Danes.

The terrain was largely clay and therefore very wet. After the first hole which ran parallel to the Warwick Road and which was subject to flooding whenever the River Avon overflowed its banks, the course climbed away from the road and was quite hilly. One particularly delightful hole was the eighth – a short hole, known as the Pulpit, with a plateau green having Chestnut trees at the back.

Activity Commences at Welcombe

The Club's activities on the new course began straight away in the spring of 1897 and during that spring and summer much work was done on the greens by the Captain Mr G F Kendall and Mr Ashwin.

On Thursday 29th April the Midland Counties Ladies' Golf

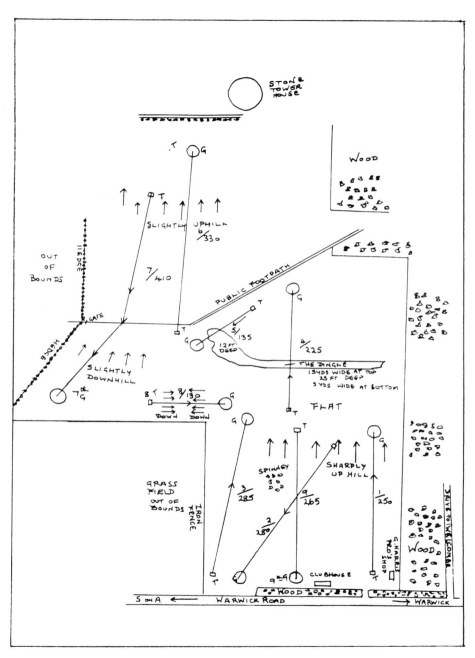

Plan of Welcombe Course – from a drawing by Ted Evans

14

Championship was held at Kings Norton Golf Club – Stratford being represented by Mrs Park, Miss Crawford and Mrs Wilson.

A hut had been provided to act as a club house for the early days. This was divided into sections – one for use of the members and the other for use by the greenkeeper. This had been purchased from Kennards at a cost of £11-8-0 and had been erected by the members.

On 1st October 1897 a robbery took place at the Golf Club. Three coats and blazers were missing from the members' portion whilst in the greenkeeper's department there were missing a silver watch chain and an umbrella. The greenkeeper Mr Herbert Fitzjohn reported 'that the building had been secured when he left at nine p.m. on Tuesday night. On Wednesday at 7-30 am he discovered that both windows had been entered, presumably in daylight as no matches were found'.

The course quickly took shape during this first year and on 10th December 1897 the following comment appeared in the Stratford Herald:

'The Stratford-on-Avon Golf Links; A correspondent of the Birmingham Post writes as follows:
"Little contradiction would probably be advanced that Stratford-upon-Avon is one of the most attractive towns in England and from a golfer's point of view, the attractiveness has been during this past few months materially enhanced, for the new course at Welcombe, laid out on the undulating banks of that nobly planned park, bids fair to take rank among our best midland links. It is emphatically a pretty course, although there is still considerable work necessary on the putting greens, but one must not expect too much in this respect of a new course. The professional engaged hails from St Andrews, and should know his work better than we can teach him in this district, and we have no doubt that this part of the ground will soon rival in excellence the fair green. Mr C V Howitt playing round there the other day in the excellent scores of (39 and 38) – 77, came in two below the professional record of the green."
The fourth AGM (the first since the course at Welcombe was opened) was held on 14th January 1898 at the Union Club. The

15

accounts showed an adverse balance at the beginning of the year of £9-17-10. Principal items of expenditure during the year were £30-0-0 wages for the professional and £10-00 rent. The year end adverse balance was £26-15-6. Mr G F Kendall was again re-elected Captain and Mr G C Lowndes Hon. Secretary. Both offered to stand down as soon as better people were available. There were expressions of thanks to Mr Kendall and Mr Ashwin for the work they had done on the greens.

Mr Kendall had presented a Challenge Cup for the gentlemen and Mr Lowndes similarly for the ladies. Both cups being very handsome. Mr Wilson had won the Men's and it was presented to him by Mr Kendall, the recipient expressing his personal thanks and also the thanks of the Club for the generosity of the donor. The Ladies' Cup was won by Miss M Holtom. She was not present to receive it, but Miss Crawford expressed the thanks of the ladies to Mr Lowndes for his kindness.

On 20th May 1898 the following report appeared in the Stratford-upon-Avon Herald:

'We are pleased to note the advance the Stratford-on-Avon Golf Club is making both as regards its membership and the number of prizes to be played for. A handsome pair of candlesticks, the gift of Sir Arthur Hodgson, have already been secured by a lady member, and there is the Hon Secretary's Ladies' Challenge Medal Cup in the hands of another member. Sir George and Lady Trevelyan are giving a silver bowl as a Ladies' Bogey Challenge Prize, which we understand will shortly be on view in Mr Pierce's window in Bridge Street. The conditions regarding the competition are not, however, at the moment to hand. Added to this we hear of a second prize coming in the same direction. The gentlemen have not been forgotten. There is a Captain's Medal Challenge Cup adorning the shelf of a reverend gentleman, and we hear also that Mr Sanders of Alveston Manor, has announced his intention of giving a silver cup to be played for under handicap of strokes, to be retained by any member winning it three times consecutively, to be played for not less than three times within twelve months. We express a hope that we may in the future be told of a bogey challenge prize to be competed for, and there we think the club will be well off indeed. The wise move the committee of management made, when they gave up distant Wilmcote and opened the present pretty links at Welcombe, is bringing forth its expected fruit. at the same time we must remember that the basis of the present position of the club is largely due to the energy of a lady member whose untiring efforts are being crowned with this success'. (Identity not disclosed – Author).

During 1898 the gentlemen played matches against Leamington and Broadway, both resulting in a whitewash for Stratford, but the ladies had their revenge for an earlier defeat of 48 holes to nil by beating Leamington 16 holes to 4 on January 28th.

At the AGM held on 14th February 1899, the President Sir George Trevelyan presented a handsome Silver Bowl to the Ladies Section to be competed for in a Bogey Competition. Mr G F Kendall was again elected Captain and a special sub-committee was formed to look into the provision of a Clubhouse.

Steady progress was maintained during 1899 with much work carried out to improve the quality of the greens and the course generally.

In September Arthur Fowler was appointed Greenkeeper/ Professional, and a match was arranged to take place on 1st January 1900 between him and J Cooper of Ealing. 'Both men being sterling exponents of the game and an interesting struggle was expected'.

Firm Progress by the Club

On 14th February 1900 the Club held its sixth AGM. This meeting was reported very fully in the Stratford Herald of 16th February 1900 and makes very interesting reading, including an entertaining speech by the President, Sir George Trevelyan.

17

STRATFORD-ON-AVON GOLF CLUB.
SPEECH BY SIR GEORGE TREVELYAN.

The annual meeting of the Stratford Golf Club took place at the Union club, on Wednesday afternoon. The president (Sir George Trevelyan) took the chair, and there were also present the Mayor (Mr. W. Pearce), the Rev. H. Wilson, Mr. S. Sanders, Mr. Bird, Mr. B Norbury, Dr. Thomson, Mr. G. F. Kendall (captain), Mr. C. Lowndes (hon. secretary), Miss Hodgson, Miss Crawford, Mrs. Thomson, Miss Holtom, Mrs. New, Mrs. Stevenson, and the Misses Ashwin. Letters apologising for non-attendance were announced from the Vicar (the Rev. G. Arbuthnot), and Mr. Sargeant, of Henley - in - Arden, while the hon. secretary announced that Mr. Green had resigned his membership of the club.

A BALANCE ON THE RIGHT SIDE.

Mr. Lowndes, in presenting the financial statement, said they commenced the year with an overdraft at the bank of £11 18s 4d. During the year they had received 77 subscriptions at £1 1s and ten at half-a-guinea, from visitors (monthly, weekly, and daily) £4 0s 6d, and the sale of one key had brought in 1s. The principal item of expenditure was the payment of professionals, £40 15s, and there was a balance in hand of £12 3s 5d—(applause).

Mr. Norbury proposed that the accounts be passed, remarking that the statement was in every way satisfactory.

Mr. Bird seconded, and it was agreed to.

On the motion of the Chairman, seconded by Mr. Kendall, Viscount Lifford was added to the list of vice-presidents.

ELECTION OF OFFICERS.

Mr. Sanders proposed the re-election of Mr. Kendall as captain for the ensuing year. Mr. Kendall had been captain ever since the formation of the club, and he (the speaker) could vouch that he had taken a great amount of personal interest in the club. On the captain devolved the arranging of the matches, and Mr. Kendall had always carried out the duties of that responsible position to the satisfaction of the members—(hear, hear). He should like to mention one matter in the accounts. He understood that during the year they had purchased half-a-wheelbarrow—(laughter) As they now had a balance on the right side he hoped during the ensuing 12 months they would buy the other half—(laughter)—and that it would be used for getting rid of the mud which came from off the rollers on to the greens. It was very perplexing and depressing to a player making what he thought would prove a pretty approach stroke to the green to find that the mud on the green scraped from the roller had stopped the ball, and turned it either to the right or the left, with the result that the golf player had to make two or more additional strokes. He trusted that between the secretary, treasurer, and captain this would be attended to.

Miss Hodgson, as representing the Ladies' Committee, said that the ladies' tees were not quite in order. The tee that a player approached on driving up to the fence was in a terrible state, and she hoped that the professional's attention would be called to it.

The Rev. H. Wilson seconded the re-appointment of Mr. Kendall, testifying to that gentleman's value as captain and the great interest he took in the game.

The motion was carried unanimously, and Mr. Kendall, in returning thanks, said he must plead guilty to having filled the position of captain for several years. As soon as they could find a better man he should be willing to stand aside, and he hoped that personage would soon arrive. He had taken note of the little remarks made, and he would try and get the defects remedied as soon as possible. With regard to the tee mentioned by Miss Hodgson, he thought it had been recently moved further back, but he would see that it was rolled.

On the proposition of the Mayor, Mr. C. E. Martin was re-elected hon. treasurer.

The Chairman hoped he was acting in accordance with custom, but certainly with a desire that his motion would be agreed to, in moving the re-election of Mr. Lowndes as hon. secretary—(applause).

Miss Hodgson seconded, remarking that they could not have found a more energetic or better-tempered secretary than Mr. Lowndes.

Mr. Lowndes, in returning thanks, said it would give him pleasure to continue to act as their hon. secretary during the last year of the present century, in the hope that they would obtain an ideal secretary to start the new century with, one who had more time at his disposal.

Mr. Stevenson was re-appointed hon. auditor, and on the motion of Miss Hodgson, seconded by Mrs. Thomson, Miss Crawford was again chosen as hon. secretary to the ladies' committee.

The old committee, the Rev. H. Wilson, Dr. Thomson, and Messrs Ashwin, Airth Richardson, A. B. Sanders, and Stevenson, were re-elected, and on the proposition of Mr. Kendall Mr. T. F. Beetson was elected a member of the club.

THE CLUB'S PERFORMANCES.

Mr. Kendall said that during the year the Club had played 14 matches, scoring 255 holes, while 197 holes had been registered against them, leaving a margin of 58 holes in their favour—(applause) If it had not been for one most unfortunate match, which was played in an impenetrable fog—(laughter)—and in which the score more resembled a cricket than a golf match—(renewed laughter)—they would have been 125 holes to the good, but that one game knocked them down more than he cared to specify. The previous year they played 10 matches and registered but 149 holes, having 179 holes scored against them, so they might congratulate themselves on the improvement in their play. The Clubs they had met had also been stronger. They had played teams like Olton, Kenilworth, and Blackwell, and when the list was first made out it was thought that they would fare very badly indeed. However, that had not been the case. The Captain's Cup had been won by Mr. W. F. Hutchings with a score of 237, his three rounds resulting 82 79 76, a very good record indeed—(hear, hear). Mr. D. B. Sanders was second with a score of 250, Dr. Thomson third with 251, and Mr. A. B. Sanders fourth with 257 It was gratifying to note that these four scores were all better than the four best totals of the previous year, when Mr. W. F. Hutchings headed the list with a score of 258. The Sanders' Cup was won in March by Mr. Stevenson with a score of 85, and in October by Mr. Hutchings with 83. He had to express his thanks to Mr. A. B. Sanders for his services in arranging the matches. Mr. Sanders was well-known in golf circles in the Midlands, and through his agency the club had been able to compile a superior list of fixtures. Mr. Sanders had also attended every match, and nearly

AGM report – Stratford Herald
16th February 1900

18

always won his game. In the summer the club had had to stop playing for a time owing to the haymaking. He could promise nothing definite for this season, although efforts would be made to arrange that play might be carried on, over some of the holes at any rate. They wanted a bogey prize very badly, and he hoped some day they would get one. If they obtained more prizes it would be possible to combine two or three meetings, and have a summer meeting, when the prizes would be played for—(applause). In his opinion such an event would do a lot to encourage golf. In conclusion, he wished to express his obligations to all playing members, especially to the outside members, such as Mr. Sargeant and Mr. Payton, who came good distances to participate in the games. On the whole the outlook was very promising. Certainly the play had very much improved, and a good deal of keenness was displayed by the members. He was sorry to say that they were losing such good players as Mr. A. B. Sanders and Mr. W. F. Hutchings for twelve months, so it was possible that the ensuing season would not be so successful.

Mr. LOWNDES said that since the club was instituted at Welcombe it had progressed; before that time the membership began to fall off on account of the distance from the railway. The present holder of the President's and Lady Trevelyan's silver challenge bowl was Miss Alice Holtom, while the Captain's cup passed from Mr. B. Norbury to Mr. W. F. Hutchings. The hon. secretary's challenge cup was in the careful hands of Mrs. Park. The mixed foursomes, arranged by the ladies, were very much appreciated, and the present holders were the Rev. O. Mordaunt and Miss M. Allfrey. He understood that this competition would be played again in the spring.

The MAYOR proposed a hearty vote of thanks to Sir George Trevelyan for his conduct in the chair. They were all delighted to see Sir George amongst them—(applause), and a short while back he (the Mayor) saw their president, with his golfing implements, walking over the links. He was glad to find that Sir George was not a sleeping member, and trusted that he would remain for many years as president of the club.

Mr. S. SANDERS seconded, and referring to the closing words of the Mayor, said he would suggest to their esteemed chairman that the way to continue in office as their president for some time to come was to stick to the game of golf—(laughter and applause). Some people got discouraged when they started to play, especially when they began late in life, but it was really amazing how soon and imperceptibly one improved in the game—(hear, hear). Golf, too, had a wonderful effect in prolonging life. He knew of an old gentleman of 78, who had to carry over the links 18 stone and upwards in addition to his golfing implements—(laughter), and he declared that he would never have survived so long had it not been for the pastime of golf.

The motion was carried with acclamation.

Sir GEORGE TREVELYAN, who, on rising, said it gave him very great pleasure to be present on that occasion. He could not help but think, on such an afternoon as that, that people must possess a very strong imagination to assemble together and discuss golf, a game that before everything was connected with the green turf—(laughter). The members of that club were certainly very heroic. Lady Trevelyan was passing the links on Saturday, and informed him that she saw the game being played under climatic circumstances that required very exceptional bravery. The financial state of the club was a source of great satisfaction to him—(hear, hear).

He had in his time heard many budgets read, he trembled to say how many, but seldom had he heard one of so satisfactory a nature as that presented by the hon. secretary that afternoon. He always considered that no man of business should take part in a concern or institution which did not pay its way. The first business in his opinion of a Board—he was not alluding to Companies but to institutions—was to see that the receipts covered the expenses, and he would never remain connected with a body that did not do all in its power to keep in a sound financial state. The Golf Club began the year £10 behind, but finished £10 in front—(hear, hear). They also had some wonderful assets, a roller for every green—(laughter)—and, he understood, a wheelbarrow and a half — (renewed laughter). That was an extraordinary state of things, and he hoped they would continue to follow the golden precept, laid down by Mr. Micawber, of always keeping ahead of your expenditure by never letting your expenses exceed your income—(hear, hear). He felt that he had no right to be their President, but he had learnt from experience that very often prominent places were given to those who were ill-fitted to fill them. He had heard the position admirably described by Mr. Cobden, who once remarked that at a meeting of an agricultural society a lord or a member of Parliament was put in the chair. He began his speech by saying that he was the only man in the assembly who knew nothing about agriculture, and his was the only speech reported in the newspaper—(laughter). He stood in the same position with regard to the game of golf. At present his great ambition was to go round the links with a less number of strokes than would total the years of his life, but he knew that achievement was beyond fruition. But as a golfer who played so badly, who learnt the game so recently, and yet loved it so well, he was perhaps qualified to say a word about the beauty of the ground—which it would be certainly hard to surpass—a spot which was full of historical associations. Where could they find another ground from which could be seen three objects like Charlecote, the spire of dear old Stratford church, and Edge Hill, three pictures so beautiful and famous in literature and history—(applause). He could never forget that those very bunkers from which the poor golfer extricated his ball with so much difficulty—(laughter)—formed the self-same dingles that Shakespeare would never have enclosed—(applause) — and he took good care to make arrangements with the lord of the manor to secure this. He was glad that both Lady Trevelyan and himself were now able to spend a larger portion of their time there. They loved the place and country better every year, and were always pleased to do anything that would be of the slightest service to the town of which they were so proud, and to the neighbours with whom they felt such an amount of friendship and goodwill—(applause).

Mixed Foursomes

About this time the Ladies' Section promoted a Mixed Foursome event, for which the ladies had presented a trophy. This event was played for the second time in March 1900 and took place on a Wednesday in bright sunny weather. It was won by Miss Crawford and Mr Peyton who held the trophy until November when it was played for again. It had been won on the first occasion by Miss Allen and the Rev O Mordaunt.

On Boxing Day 1900 the ladies organised a Mixed Foursome event open to members and friends staying with them. Mrs A D Flower had presented the first prize and Mrs Flower and Miss Hodgson had invited all players to lunch at the club house. The weather proved propitious and following the game the players were able to enjoy an out of door lunch so generously provided by Mrs Flower and Miss Hodgson. The winners were Miss A Holtom and Mr G F Kendall.

Club Progress

By 1901 the Club was firmly established with members having success in Open Meetings at other clubs. At Easter Mr W F Hutchings won the Smurthwaite Challenge Cup and Silver Memento at Scarborough Golf Club and Mr Brewster Norbury was amongst the top scorers at the Open Meeting at Aberdovey Golf Club.

The accounts for the year 1901 show an increase in rent from £10 to £45. A pencil note alongside refers to the land being taken over from Mr Wynne at Michaelmas 1900. No mention is made of the remainder of the course. This increase suggests that the tenancy of the land became that of the Club direct to Lady Trevelyan to whom the rent was paid in future years.

By August the Stratford Herald was reporting that 'the picturesque links at Welcombe are now in excellent order. Few visitors to Stratford are aware of the existence, close at hand, of links that are second to few in beauty of position and sporting characteristics. Daily or weekly tickets are available from Mr E Fox's, High Street'.

20

At the AGM held on 12th March 1902 Mr G F Kendall, Captain for the previous six years resigned and was succeeded by Mr J H Lloyd.

In 1902 the efforts of the Club House Sub-Committee came to fruition and the following report appeared in the Stratford Herald of 3rd October.

'That golf is losing none of its attraction in Stratford is proved by the enterprise shown by its members and friends in erecting the new club house in close proximity to Warwick Road. The old wooden hut served its purpose in the early years of the Club, but with an increased membership something better became necessary. Then again the present building is more accessible and possesses accommodation which the other lacked. Sir George and Lady Trevelyan not only handsomely contributed to the funds, but gave permission for its erection on the site it occupies, which could not be more convenient or easy of access. The building is simple enough in design, but contains all the essentials of a club house. A verandah runs the whole length of the front, which can be used for witnessing the game when play takes place on that part of the links. The centre room is bright and commodious, and on each side is a dressing room with the customary lockers. In the rear is a pantry with the necessary appliances for providing tea on match days, and, perhaps in the course of time the provisioning department may be extended. As cycling will, doubtless, be much resorted to for reaching the links, accommodation has been made at the back for members' machines. General brightness characterises the building both inside and out, and the club may be congratulated in its latest important accession. It is appropriately designed and solidly built, and to Mr James Cox of Rother Street, credit is due for the admirable manner in which the work is carried out.'

By 1903 the club house account was showing an overdraft of £58-2-0 and the Captain Mr J H Lloyd and the Hon Secretary Mr C H Lowndes had signed a guarantee to the bank for £50-00. At the AGM held on 18th February 1903 it was agreed that this debt should be wiped off as soon as possible and members who had not subscribed were asked to do so immediately, now that they had seen and recognised the advantage of having a building available.

The Club House at Welcombe Fields 1905.

The Warwick Road near Welcombe Fields 1905.
Photos: J Humphreys

At this meeting an entrance fee of £1-1-0 for all new members was introduced. Mr Lloyd was re-elected Captain.

During the next three years the club house deficit was steadily reduced and stood at £18-1-6 at the end of 1906. Mr D B Sanders had succeeded Mr J H Lloyd as Captain and was Captain from 1904 until he left Stratford-upon-Avon in April 1906. Mr Brewster Norbury then took over as Captain and was confirmed in that position when elected at the AGM on 11th March 1907.

At this meeting a presentation was made to the Hon Secretary Mr C H Lowndes, of a silver tea tray, subscribed for by the members, in token of his service in the previous ten years.

Mr Brewster Norbury continued as Captain in 1907 and 1908 and brought his handicap down to Plus 2 by the beginning of 1908.

1909–1914. The Five Years Prior to the First World War

By 1909 the Club was firmly established at the Welcombe, and a pattern of events and play had been gradually developing. At the AGM of that year a major item of contention was the use of the Club premises on Sunday. It was proposed that the Club premises be not used on Sundays, in any event not before 12-30 pm and after 6-30 pm. This proposal was defeated, and the vicar, the Rev W G Melville stated that his golfing days at Stratford would be at an end.

Mr Archibald Flower gave permission to play through his field 'The Spyford'.

In 1909, a new member joined the Club – Mr Guy Pemberton who was to prove a great asset in later years. He was elected Captain in 1911, remained Captain for 10 years, and was very involved in keeping the Club going in the four years of World War 1.

In 1912 a letter was received from Sir George Trevelyan resigning as President after 14 years, due to a need to restrict his activities. A resolution was passed at the AGM, unanimously expressing sincere appreciation of the great services he had rendered to the Club during the previous fourteen years and deep gratitude for his kind and thoughtful interest in the welfare of the Club. Mr F M Hodgson (Vice President) was elected President to succeed Sir George, and Mr Archibald Flower was elected Vice President.

In 1913 and 1914 respectively 'Bogey' Cups were presented by Mr Ludford Docker for the men and by Mr G C Lowndes for the ladies, both cups to be competed for under similar rules.

During 1913, Mr George Harris became the Club's professional, and at the AGM on 22 January 1914 Mr Lowndes paid tribute to his good services.

The First World War 1914–1918

The outbreak of war in August 1914 and the consequent exodus of members and staff, volunteers called to the colours, presented those remaining with many difficulties in keeping the Club going and the links in good order.

The professional Mr George Harris took over the sub-tenancy for grazing rights for an annual fee of £32.

By the end of 1915 membership was Men 50 and Ladies 34. The budget of September 1915 had raised Schedule B Taxation (Land Charge) from £1-18-9 to £7-19-9. This heavy land charge emphasised the Club's debt to the Mayor, Mr A D Flower, for his generosity in allowing a field enclosing two greens to be played over rent-free.

In August 1916 G A Harris (professional) was called to the colours. It was agreed that his position would be kept open for him on return, should the Club be still in existence, and that his grazing sub tenancy would continue. Mrs Harris was employed to look after the club house, green fees, canteen, payment of wages and insurance cards, at a weekly wage of 10/-. An assistant (Farr) was kept on to look after the general upkeep of the links at 16/- per week. A half share in the wages of a boy (Butler) at 8/- per week, Harris to pay 4/- and the club 4/-, who was employed to help Farr in the afternoon.

A gift of a wristwatch was made to Harris and members were asked to subscribe 2/6 each. This resulted in a sum of £6-7-6 being collected, and after purchase of a wristwatch (a good one) and a leather purse a sum of £3/3/- was handed to Harris with the presents.

In October 1916 a Notice of Assessment under Schedule B of Income Tax Act for year ending April 1917 for £11-5-0 was received.

24

G A Harris – The Club's first professional.
Photo: Molly Moore

Five shillings in the pound duty was chargeable against the rent of £45-00. The Club appealed but was turned down, no relief being granted as long as the Club were the direct tenants. It was therefore proposed to make the tenancy over to Harris to circumvent this, but Sir George Trevelyan did not like this proposal. He wrote a letter to the committee saying, 'That as an old Public Man he did not like the idea of making the tenancy over to Harris with the sole object of evading this tax. He thought that more than ever, everyone should do their utmost to pay these extra charges we were called on to bear and that must be the first thought of all in these matters.'

By November 1917 a serious financial situation had developed. The Club was overdrawn £38-00 and it was estimated this would rise to £50-00–£60-00 by the year end.

The Club approached Sir George and Lady Trevelyan asking if during the period of the War they could see their way clear to accepting a payment of only half the rent, £22-10-00 instead of £45-00.

This request was turned down and Sir George wrote back suggesting that because of the serious financial state of the Club and the country's need for food production the course should be ploughed up, and the Club disbanded.

This and two further letters from Sir George were considered by the General Committee on 12th January 1918 and it was decided to continue with the Golf Club and to economise by wages reduction from 10/- to 5/- for Harris and only keeping the boy (Butler) on the staff, and to accept an offer from Sir Archibald Flower to reduce the rent for the 'Blue Cap' field, and the use of a horse free of charge from G A Harris. The Secretary wrote to Sir George accordingly. Sir George replied offering reduction of £5-00 rent in March and September 1918 and wishing the Club success and prosperity, but both he and Lady Trevelyan wished to resign from membership of the Club.

By early 1918 the serious situation of the War and the need to maximise food production led to consideration being given to ploughing up the golf links of the county. The following article appeared in the Stratford Herald of 4th January 1918, and on 23rd February the Club received notice from the War Agricultural Committee to plough up the 'Blue Cap Field'.

LOCAL AND DISTRICT NOTES.

Stratford Herald report 4th
January 1918.

GOLF LINKS IN DANGER.

Now that we are seriously endeavouring to supplement our food supplies nothing at all feasible will be allowed to stand in the way of accomplishing this task. Of course, those who derive so much enjoyment from our public pastimes will regret to see them effaced for a time, but when the national interests are in such grave peril there will be a general feeling to abandon everything that menaces our food resources. The matter of ploughing up the golf links of the county has again engaged the attention of the War Agricultural Committee, but before this extreme measure is resorted to full authority has to be obtained from high quarters. Various matters have to be considered in connection with such a proceeding. These much-favoured places have had expended upon them considerable labour in preparation, involving, of course, no small expenditure of money. Doubtless their owners would receive compensation for disturbance, but in some instances the price to be paid might have to be submitted to arbitration. Therefore, the question is one that cannot be determined off-hand, and some little delay may be necessary before the final resolve is made. The Committee, fortunately, has large powers conferred upon it, but there is no wish to deal arbitrarily with such important questions.

THE GOLF CLUB.—We are pleased to learn that the local club has successfully weathered the storm of the last four years, and is in a fairly satisfactory financial position, due chiefly to the cutting down of all expenses to a minimum and the generosity exhibited on the part of the two landlords. It has, of course, meant that the fairway has had to "go," but most of the greens and tees have been kept in fairly good trim. The committee now realise the importance of getting all into first class order again as soon as possible, so when the weather improves and additional labour can be obtained it is their intention to restore it to its former excellent condition, as they realise that a good Golf Club is absolutely essential to a town catering as ours does for visitors. It is hoped that the professional, George Harris, who has been serving in France, will soon be able to return and assume his duties. An open meeting will be held during the coming year, and the Club competitions started as soon as possible. Attention may be called to a notice in our advertising columns.

Stratford Herald report
24th January 1919

In August Sir George and Lady Trevelyan offered to release the Club from its tenancy agreement. On 3rd September a letter was sent replying that the Club intended to carry on. There was greater use of the links and it was important to keep the Club alive for the benefit of its members serving in the forces and for American forces visitors on leave. The aim was to provide free golf for all allied forces on leave.

By the end of 1918 the War was over. In May 1919 G C Harris, now demobilized, came back to the Club, this time as Professional and manager of the links at a salary of 30/- per week, temporarily raised to 40/-, until such time as he was able to give more lessons and make more clubs, when it would revert to 30/-.

Butler was to be paid 20/-, raised to 22/- from 2nd June and Harris was instructed to find a third man as soon as possible.

The Post War Era

This then was the setting in which the Club began to pick itself up after four years of war, during which it had been kept going by the efforts of a number of members, in particular Mr Guy Pemberton, the Captain, and Mr G C Lowndes, Hon Secretary.

There had been no General Meeting of members since the AGM of 25th January 1916. In June 1919 a special General Meeting was requested by ten members to know the financial position, elect committee and officers and to discuss improvements and extensions to the links.

This meeting was held on 8th July 1919. Financial statements for the years 1916, 1917 and 1918 were presented. An adverse balance of £42-7-2 at the end of 1917 had been improved in 1918 to a balance in hand of £5-9-11.

A further Special General Meeting was held on 21st November 1919 to receive a report of the Green Committee and to consider proposed alterations to the course, plans of which has been on view in the club house. Regrettably a copy of this plan had not been found, but the detailed alterations were as follows: 'To form a new green in a hollow on the face of the bank below the first green. This would do away with the present bad and blind first hole. The old eighth green would then become the new second and will make a good open hole; the tee for it being just above the new first green.' These proposals were adopted and a Course Improvement Fund started. Donations from members were requested and a sum of £79-12-0 was raised from these donations.

The 23rd AGM was held on 24th January 1920. The financial statement (see page 31) showed an adverse balance of £64-10-10, largely due to the cost of bringing the links up to standard after five years of making do. The main item of expenditure was £237–8–19 for labour.

Mr Guy Pemberton was re-elected Captain and Mr G C Lowndes resigned office as Hon Secretary after 23 years' service. Gifts were presented to Mr Lowndes, subscribed to by members. Mr Lowndes was then elected a Life Member of the Club. A report appeared in the Stratford Herald of 24th January 1920, and mistakenly reported that Mr Lowndes had been made an Honorary Member.

Mr G C Evans was elected Hon Secretary to succeed Mr Lowndes.

Subscriptions were set at	£3-3-0 Men	£1-11-6 Ladies.
Entrance Fees	£3-3-0 Men	£1-11-6 Ladies.
Green Fees	2/-	Monday–Friday
	2/-	Saturday or Sunday am
	3/-	Whole Day Saturday or Sunday
	10/-	Per Week
	25/-	Per Month.

Half Fees to relatives or members non resident.

In March 1920 it was agreed to pay Harris £3-0-0 per annum for the use of his horse during the winter, then in October a new agreement was made with Harris to exclude cattle and horses from the course between the months of October and April.

By 1921 the financial position had improved to a balance in hand of £2-18-11 due largely to the increased subscriptions and green fees and in April it was decided to buy a mowing machine for £32-00 less whatever discount could be obtained.

At the AGM in February 1922 a Contingency Fund was created of £50-00. A canteen attendant was taken on at a wage of 10/- per

Stratford-on-Avon Golf Club.

December 11th, 1919.

Dear Sir or Madam,

Since the Special General Meeting on November 22nd when the proposed alterations to the course were adopted, your Green Committee, having regard to certain suggestions made at the meeting, have given additional consideration to the contemplated improvements.

They have adopted a suggestion to form a new 1st Green in a hollow on the face of the bank below the present 1st Green. This will do away with the present bad and blind 1st hole. The old 8th Green will then become the new second and will make a good open hole, the tee for it being just above the new 1st Green.

A Plan showing the final scheme of the alterations can be seen in the Club House.

As the Club funds will show a deficit of approximately £60 at the end of the current year, it is decided to start a "Course Improvement Fund" with which to defray the cost of these alterations, until such a time as the finances of the Club are able to shoulder the burden. Our present intention, therefore, is to proceed bit by bit with the alterations and general improvements, taking care that the general funds of the Club shall not be called upon. The permanent Ground Staff will also be reduced from four to three in order to help the Club debt.

Donations have already been promised, but more will be required, and we therefore ask for your kind help in order that the course may be put into more attractive form as soon as possible. Donations should be sent to Mr. Knill, the Hon. Treasurer, Old Bank, Stratford-on-Avon.

The following have already been promised :—

	£	s.	d.		£	s.	d.
A. D. Flower	12	0	0	Guy Pemberton	1	1	0
L. C. Docker	5	5	0	Mrs. Park	1	1	0
Sir Whitworth Wallis ...	3	3	0	G. C. Evans	1	1	0
Rev. F. H. Hodgson ...	3	3	0	T. F. Norbury	1	1	0
B. Norbury	3	3	0	A. J. Knill	1	1	0
F. Winter	3	3	0	C. Lowndes	1	1	0
Percy Gem	3	3	0	S. B. Walker	1	1	0
Mr. and Mrs. Hilder ...	2	2	0	G. H. Payton	1	1	0

GUY PEMBERTON, Captain.

C. LOWNDES, Hon. Secretary.

A. J. KNILL, Hon. Treasurer.

Letter to members 11th December 1919

GOLF CLUB. – The annual meeting of the members was held at the Union Club on Saturday week, the President (the Rev. F. H. Hodgson) in the chair, and thirty-one members, including six ladies, being present. The financial statement was read, and its adoption was moved by the President and seconded by Mr. P. Winterton. The statement showed an adverse balance of £64 10s 10d, this being largely due to the upkeep of the links, an item of £237 8s 10d, made up chiefly of labour in bringing them into condition after five years of semi-neglect. For the office of captain, Mr. Evans proposed that Mr. Guy Pemberton be once more elected to this responsible and not easy post, and this was seconded by Mr. A. J. Knill, and duly carried. Mr. Pemberton, in replying, reviewed the past year, and also spoke in rosy terms of the future when the present improvements were completed. He also remarked that the club was very short of challenge cups, and invited any member or other public body that might feel inclined to present one. The President then informed the meeting that Mr. Chas. Lowndes was resigning the hon. secretaryship after a service extending over twenty-three years, during which time he had, by his courtesy and consideration of others, made himself beloved by all, and it was with the greatest possible pleasure that he had to hand to him in the name of some sixty of the members a few gifts, comprising the Victoria History of Warwickshire in two volumes, together with a crocodile blotter and pocket book, as a small expression of the esteem they all felt for him. Mr. Lowndes thanked the members for the gifts, remarking that he should prize them very highly. Owing to his age he felt that he should make way to a younger man. Mr. Lowndes was then, upon the proposition of Mr. Pemberton, elected an honorary member of the Club. Upon the proposition of Mr. Pemberton, Mr. G. C. Evans was elected hon. secretary, and in tendering his thanks for the distinction conferred on him, he asked for the co-operation of every member to help in making the club a success. Mr. A. J. Knill was re-elected hon. treasurer upon the proposal of the President, seconded by Mr. Lowndes, and supported by Mr. P. Winterton. The committee were then elected, the following coming out first in the ballot :—Mrs. Park, Sir W. Wallis, Messrs T. F. Norbury, S. B. Walker, F. D. Spencer, and H. W. Bainbridge. The alterations of rules 7 and 11 were discussed, and it was finally decided to raise the subscriptions for men to £3 3s, for ladies £1 11s 6d, with an increased entrance fee of £3 3s for men and £1 11s 6d for ladies as from June next. The new scale of visitors' fees was also adopted. A hearty vote of thanks to the President terminated the proceedings.

Stratford Herald report 24th
January 1920

Statement of Receipts and Expenditure.

YEAR ENDING 31st DECEMBER, 1919.

Receipts.		£	s.	d.	Expenditure.		£	s.	d.
1919.					1919.				
Jan. 1	By Balance in Bank	5	9	11	Dec. 31	To Rents, less Grazings	26	0	0
Dec. 31	„ Subscriptions	159	11	6		„ Rates and Taxes	25	17	8
	„ Entrance Fees	22	1	0		„ Upkeep of Links	237	8	10
	„ Visitors' Fees	53	6	0		„ Ditto Club House	17	0	6
	„ Locker Rents	7	15	0		„ Sundries	12	14	1
	„ Profit on Sales (2 years)	4	11	10		„ Bank Interest (*nil*)	—		
	„ Medals Account	1	15	0					
	„ Balance due to Bank	64	10	10					
		£319	1	1			£319	1	1

January 10th, 1920.

Financial statement year ending
31st December 1919

week; the balance to be paid by Harris out of his commission. Harris to take any profit from the service of tea.

In the summer of 1922 Harris, the professional, engaged an assistant, John Humphreys. One of his tasks was to look after the caddies. The fee for caddies in those days was one shilling and two pence for two rounds of the nine hole course. They then had to clean and polish the clubs.

Wooden clubs at that time had the head spliced on to the shaft and in a hot summer the glue would soften and frequently the head of the club would come adrift and follow the ball down the fairway. A green Dunlop ball was a floating ball – slightly larger than the standard ball – probably about the size of today's ball, and were used on such holes as the sixth where there was a pond and so could be easily retrieved.

Grass Cutting

At Welcombe there was no tractor and the new mowing machine was drawn by horse. The Club had two war horses, one of which was blind. The fairways were cut in this fashion until the horses were pensioned off and given to a farmer some years later when the Club moved to Tiddington Road. The rough was cut by a local farmer in Snitterfield, William Palmer, father of Gus Palmer, a current member of long standing. He would send some men down from Snitterfield with four horses and two haymaking machines and cut the rough. Gus often helped by raking back in the corners of the field to clear the cut hay from that still standing and so help to make a tidy cut. The cut hay was then taken away by men from Flowers brewery, to be used for the brewery horses.

Gus had his reward for his help by being allowed to go to the course with his friend on a Saturday morning, pay six pence to hire a few clubs and play the course as much as they wished. Gus was eleven years old and after playing they were allowed into the club house to buy a drink of Vimto.

Expansion and Improvement of the Club

It was now the summer of 1922 and the Club had recovered well after the years of war. Consideration was being given to extending the course to 18 holes and an approach was made to Lady Trevelyan as to the possibility of renting the 'Parks'. She replied declining this proposal in a letter to Sir Whitworth Wallis dated 22nd May 1922. (See page 34 – unfortunately part of the original is missing).

Later in the same year a site on the other side of the River Avon between the Banbury Road and Loxley Lane was investigated. Plans and estimates of cost of purchase were drawn up. These were considered at a Committee meeting on 11th October 1922, and the meeting was adjourned for a report on a site at Barasett. On 23rd October the meeting resumed. A letter from Hutchings & Deer putting forward a price of £4500 for the Barasett House together with seven and a half acres of adjoining parkland was considered. The project was abandoned because of the price and the distance from Stratford. The Hon Sec Mr G C Evans was asked to make enquiries into another suitable site.

Plans for a course on 155 acres of land offered by Mr Reading for £1300 were considered on 13th December 1922. After full discussion this was turned down and the Hon Secretary asked to carry out further investigation.

The 26th AGM was held on 29th January 1993 and a full report was given to the members regarding the steps that had been taken to increase the Welcombe course to 18 holes and to find a suitable alternative site. George Harris was elected a Life Member of the Club in recognition of devoted service over a period of 22 years.

The contingency fund stood at £161-7-6 and it was decided to expend some of this in alterations to the club house. Estimates had been received and finally one of £225 was accepted from Cox & Co.

The wages bill for the Club at the end of 1922 was:

Harris	£2-0-0 per week
Ryman	£2-5-0 per week
Butler	£1-17-6 per week
Miss Neal	10-0 per week

WELCOMBE,
STRATFORD ON AVON.

May 22 –
1922

Dear Sir Whitworth Wallis

I have read the papers you left with me, & I must begin by saying what a real pleasure & satisfaction it is to me, & to Sir George, to be able to help the Golf Club by letting them the present ground; & also to know that it is thoroughly suitable for the purpose, & that they are prospering.

I can assure the Com⁻ⁿ that I have no intention of

Letter from Lady Trevelyan 22nd May 1922.

34

Negotiation and Construction of a New Course at Tiddington Road

The next two years were quite momentous. First the Club was converted into a Company, limited by guarantee, and secondly a new course was constructed at Tiddington Road. In February 1924, an offer of land at Alveston Manor Farm had been made by Mr Reading, at £35 per acre for back land and 1/9 and 1/0 for frontages. Alternatively a rent of 40/- per acre on a 21 year lease. The Committee engaged Mr J H Taylor, golf course architect to survey the land to ascertain suitability and cost of layout. In the event of a favourable report a Special General Meeting would be held in the Town Hall on 7th March 1924. On 1st March the Hon Secretary was asked to contact a number of prominent businessmen in the town to meet the Committee in the Golden Lion Hotel on 5th March.

The membership list was declared closed until further notice.

The meeting duly took place on 5th March at which it was agreed that the Club rent the land at Alveston Manor Farm for 21 years with an option to purchase anytime during the tenure, such option to be exercised at the first opportunity, and in the event of a Company being formed, Ordinary Shares only to be issued.

The Special General Meeting of members was held on 7th March. Forty members were present and the proposal to construct an 18 hole course on Alveston Manor Farm was agreed. Terms were a 21 year lease with option to purchase 138 acres from Mr Reading for £4830 and 11½ acres from the Randalls Charity Trustees on a 21 year lease with an option to purchase for £800. Taylor and Hawkins had reported that the site and soil were eminently suitable for the construction of a first class golf course.

Other parties were however interested in purchasing this land and the options expired the next day. To secure the land Mr Ludford Docker came forward at the eleventh hour and offered to lend the purchase money to the Club. (A full report of this appeared in the Stratford-upon-Avon Herald on 27th March 1925 in the report on the AGM. (see page 41)). A Construction Committee was elected to see it through.

35

Mr Ludford Docker

Conversion to Limited Company and Final Days at Welcombe

An Extraordinary General Meeting was held on 29th May 1924 at which Stratford-on-Avon Golf Club was converted into Stratford-on-Avon Golf Club Ltd. An issue of Debentures was agreed of £7500 and each male member was asked to subscribe a minimum of £10.

Mr Ludford Docker was elected President.

A vote of thanks was expressed to Messrs Fieldhouse and Docker for their help in purchasing Manor Farm.

The Construction Sub-Committee consisting of Messrs B Norbury, G Pemberton, Dr P Wells and G C Evans met frequently in June and by the beginning of July a contract for construction of the new course had been agreed with Messrs J Carter & Co. They objected to cattle and sheep grazing and so the Hon Secretary was instructed to terminate the grazing agreement with G Harris and to agree suitable terms.

First Board Meeting

On Monday 7th August 1924 the first board meeting of the Stratford-on-Avon Golf Club Ltd was held at Bridge House Stratford-upon-Avon. It was reported that the Company had been duly registered and that the Certificate of Registration was dated 12th July 1924. The Committee as appointed by the articles of association then took office and Dr Wells was confirmed as Chairman.

There was a slight hitch when it was discovered that Mr R M Smith had been appointed to the Committee instead of Mr J M Smith. Upon the resignation of Mr R M Smith this matter was rectified and Somerest House informed. Attending this meeting was Mr Hemming of Messrs Christopher and Lodder, solicitors. He had with him the Contract of Sale entered into by Mr Ludford Docker on behalf of the Company for the acquisition of the Manor Farm lands for the sum of £4830, with a tithe charge of £25 per annum. The purchase price being reduced to £4730 owing to the exclusion of a certain portion of the land. He then submitted the following conveyance:

From Reading Bros in respect of 33 acres or thereabouts for the sum of (with an apportioned tithe charge of £12 per annum).	£1187-18-0
From John E Reading & Others in respect of 100 acres or thereabouts for the sum of	£3542-0-0
	£4730-0-0

The conveyance provided for an apportioned tithe charge of £13 per annum and a right of way to Tiddington Road, this to be 12 feet in width.

A discussion then took place as to whether the Golf Club should bear the whole of the tithe charge of £25 pa to the exclusion of the frontages purchased by Messrs Fieldhouse and Docker. This was left for further discussion.

Mortgages

A first mortgage for £4000 was made with Mr W J Fieldhouse and a second mortgage was made with Mr Ludford Docker for £1500, interest at 5% pa paid half yearly. The Company having the right to pay off on giving six months notice.

Six acres of this land were sold off to Messrs J M & R M Smith for £400 with a tithe charge of £2-2-0. The Company and buyers agreed that the Company had an option to repurchase in the event of the buyers wishing to sell in the future.

Debentures

Debentures limited to £7500 were issued, bearing interest at 5% pa and the Hon Secretary reported that he already had applications in respect of £3870. A call for 50% was agreed. A circular was agreed to be sent to all members enclosing a form of consent to transfer membership from the old to the new Club and asking for subscriptions of the minimum amount of £10 to the Debenture Fund. The assets of the old Club were transferred to the new company.

The contract for construction of the new course with Messrs Carter & Co was approved and a further £500 voted for this purpose, making a total of £3600.

The next twelve months were very hectic for the committee as activity on the construction of the new course gathered speed. In August the Silo and Dutch barns were let to Mr Reading at £5 and £10 respectively and the Right of Way was bought for £50. Advice was sought on the hay crop, grazing, cottage rent and apportionment of rates.

In September Carter & Co were asked to submit a scheme for bunkering with approximate cost. In October steps were taken to appoint a new greenkeeper at a salary of £4-00 per week. A further £300 was allotted to Carter & Co plus £100 for the construction of the Punch Bowl green at the 13th hole, and £300 for bunkers. In November a further £200 was allotted for bunkers and Mr Gault was engaged as greenkeeper. By December Carter & Co advised that the cost of the course to date was £4135.

On 8th January 1925, Mr Gault, greenkeeper was discharged.

Club House

With the course well under way the Committee now gave consideration to the club house and on 23rd April Mr Guy Pemberton was appointed architect – his remuneration being 'out of pocket' expenses not exceeding £25.

By the end of April plans for a new club house and an estimate of £794 were accepted from G Whalley & Sons and £89 agreed for heating apparatus.

In the meantime Mr Pemberton was making the necessary arrangements for demolishing the club house at Welcombe and re-erecting at Tiddington Road. £400 was agreed for this purpose, including installation of drainage and lockers. To do this the responsible members had to guarantee the £400.

Copt Heath Golf Club came forward in May 1925 with a very generous offer to allow the members the use of their Links whilst the new course at Tiddington Road was made ready.

Progress of the Course

The Committee now concentrated on the construction of the new course and gave consideration to installing water on the greens. It was decided that the financial position of the Club would not permit this feature and it was handed to the Green Committee to consider and report.

The new fairways were considered unsatisfactory, having too many weeds, and on 20th May 1925 Carter & Co were asked to meet the Committee on the course. A date for closing down the Welcombe was deferred until after Carter & Co's visit.

The course was now nearly ready and consideration was given to the opening date. Carter & Co were consulted as to the advisability of waiting until there had been some rain and the opening was provisionally fixed for 31st August 1925. On 6th August a decision was made to close the Welcombe course on Sunday 23rd

August and to open the new course at Tiddington Road on Saturday 29th August 1925.

Notice of termination of the tenancy at Welcombe was to date as from September quarter 1925 – being a six monthly tenancy expiring in March 1926.

A letter of thanks for past consideration and courtesies was sent to Lady Trevelyan.

The club house was still in course of erection and its opening was postponed until builder's operations permitted.

Last Months at Welcombe

All attention having been directed to the construction work at Tiddington Road, the affairs of the club at Welcombe had taken a back seat.

Two new lady members had joined. Firstly Mrs Simpson joined in 1924. She was to be a member for 45 years and was made a Life Member in 1955 and lived to be 100. She was known to all as 'Ma' Simpson. In 1925 Violet, her daughter, became a member and is still going strong in 1993 as this history is being written, having been a member for 68 years. Following in her mother's footsteps, Violet was made a Life Member in 1989. She was Ladies' President from 1980 to 1985.

On 21st March 1925 the first AGM of the Stratford-on-Avon Golf Club Ltd was held. Mr Ludford Docker was re-elected President and Mr Brewster Norbury elected Captain. A full report appeared in the Stratford-upon-Avon Herald on Monday 27th March 1925.

In May, Mr G C Evans resigned his position as Hon. Secretary after having filled that office for five and a half years.

Also in May, the Docker Cup was won by Mr S B S Walker for the third time in succession and as a consequence he retained the trophy in perpetuity.

In July, Mr Ludford Docker very kindly offered to present another cup to replace that won by Mr Walker. This offer was gratefully accepted by the Committee.

On opposite page – AGM report – Stratford Herald 27th March 1925

40

NEW GOLF COURSE.

AN ACQUISITION TO THE TOWN.

There was a goodly attendance at the annual meeting of the Stratford-on-Avon Golf Club, Ltd., held at the Town-hall on Saturday evening, when an optimistic note was struck by most of the speakers. Mr. Ludford Docker presided, and was supported by Dr. P. H. Wells (captain), Mr. G. C. Evans (hon. secretary), and Mr. W. E. Withnall (hon. auditor).

The committee reported that, pursuant to resolutions passed at an extraordinary general meeting of the old Club held on 29th May, 1924, a Company was registered, limited by guarantee, and negotiations were completed for the acquisition of freehold lands and buildings in the parish of Alveston for the purpose of a new golf course. Mortgages to the amount of £5,500 were raised, and applications had been received in respect of an intended debenture issue of £5,215. The assets of the old Club, which amounted to £327 16s 9d, had been transferred to the new Company. In accordance with plans prepared by Messrs Hawtree and Taylor, the committee had placed the construction of the course in the hands of Messrs James Carter and Co. This work was practically completed, and, under normal conditions, the committee considered that the course would be playable towards the end of September next. Plans for the construction of a golf house had been prepared by Mr. Guy Pemberton, and, subject to the requisite finances being raised, the work would be put in hand, with a view to being completed in time for the official opening of the new course.

The CHAIRMAN said he was very pleased to preside at the first annual meeting of the Golf Club, Ltd., particularly as they had been good enough to elect him president. They were now entering upon a very important era in the history of the Club, and the future was full of great possibilities. They had succeeded in getting a new course, which was at present being constructed, and some of the members had heard glowing accounts, not only of the playing green, but of the position of the course. Mr. J. H. Taylor, who was responsible for laying it out, had done his work extremely well, and he (Mr. Docker) had heard from an independent source that Mr. Taylor anticipated that this would prove one of the best courses in the Midlands. Messrs Carter and Co. had also made a good job of the seeding. The cost of the scheme was approximately £4,000, but that sum would have to be considerably exceeded in the future. The course was 6,325 yards in length, and there would be some very fine holes, which would ensure clever and entertaining play. It was rich in bunkers, and included some excellent hazards. The one short hole parallel to the Tiddington-road—150 yards in length—was a real beauty, and golfers would require a little cut on the ball to make it stop. Players would find the longer holes more difficult to judge, and the seventeenth, which was 540 yards long, would require particularly good shots for anyone to take it in two. The tees were wisely and conveniently placed, and could be put back if the big hitters wanted it. A good portion of the course was old turf, very firm and springy, and they would be able to play with dry feet after a shower of rain. It was very important that sufficient time should be given to the course to settle down. The greens had been extremely well laid out, undulating in places, very tricky, and quite up to date. If they visited some of the older courses they would not see better greens, and he thought they were going to be very proud of their new course. He complimented the hon. secretary and sub-committee, and mentioned Mr. Pollock, who had been acting

as secretary during Mr. Evans' unfortunate illness. He congratulated the committee on the time and attention they had given to the details of the scheme. They had had many difficulties to overcome, but they had surmounted them in a very creditable manner. They were very glad to see Mr. Evans present, and hoped he had quite recovered from his serious illness. Mr. Withnall had not only acted as hon. auditor, but had spent a great deal of time and trouble in the formation of the Company and the securing of the necessary finances. His valuable services were worthy of a hearty vote of thanks. Mr. Docker described the land, which cost £35 per acre, as a real gift, and said he had paid £55 an acre for land two miles further up the river, and not in anything like so good a position. Indeed, before the ink was dry on the document which gave them possession of the land, it could have been sold twice over—once at a handsome profit—both the prospective purchasers being well-known men in the golfing world. The success of the Club was practically assured, and he looked upon it as a great attraction to the town by reason of its situation and easy access.

Mr. CHAMP seconded the motion, which was carried.

Mr. WITHNALL then presented the income and expenditure account for the year, showing a balance of income over expenditure of £226 8s. He also made a statement on the assets and liabilities of the new Company.

In moving the adoption of the accounts, Sir WHITWORTH WALLIS said he looked upon Mr. Withnall as the saviour of the Golf Club. Further financial assistance would have to be forthcoming if they were to put up a golf house worthy of the course, as they were hoping for something better than the tin tabernacle on the Warwick-road. There were certain ancient buildings on the present site to which Mr. Pemberton had given a good deal of attention, and from the plans they had seen he hoped the members would soon be in possession of an admirable club house—not very large, perhaps, but sufficient for the present number of members, and a club house which could be extended in future. They must go in for something attractive, because some of the members would not be able to get round the very long course. Those who were nearing forty-five—(laughter)—would be content with doing nine holes and going into tea with the ladies. He should like to voice what must be in the minds of everyone, and that was their indebtedness to Mr. Ludford Docker for having come forward at a critical moment and secured the land. They knew what Mr. Docker was in the great field of sport, and in the business world. Mr. Docker was a very old friend of his, and when he heard that gentleman had been approached on the subject he said : " You need not trouble your little souls ; Mr. Docker will put up the cash." He had done so, and he hoped that Mr. Docker would act as president for many years—(applause).

Mr. LOUD seconded the motion, which was carried.

Reporting on the construction of the new course, Mr. G. C. EVANS said it was necessary to look back to February 23rd of last year, when the offer of the Manor Farm was first put before the committee. Previous to this there had been an endeavour to extend the Welcombe links in more than one direction, and in each case this had fallen through. Other sites had been inquired into, but in each instance something arose—either cost or unsuitability—which prevented its adoption. On February 23rd, 1924, the option of purchase of the Manor Farm was placed before the old committee, who recommended acceptance to a general meeting held at the Town-hall on March 7th. While approving the scheme for a new golf course, this meeting was rather timid, and suggested that they should only lease the land. As other people were in treaty, and also

41

as the option expired on the morrow, the situation became rather desperate ; but at the eleventh hour Mr. Docker came forward with an offer which resulted in Messrs Docker and Fieldhouse lending the money for purchase, thereby enabling Stratford to acquire a first-class eighteen-hole golf course—a chance which, once let go, might never have occurred again. After the purchase of the land the scheme, unfortunately, fell on evil days, and nearly collapsed. It was due to the untiring energy, optimism, and far-sightedness of some half-a-dozen business men that the whole thing was coaxed back to life, later to grow into the extraordinarily healthy state in which they now found it. The question of the actual construction of the course was left in the hands of Messrs B. Norbury, Wells, Pemberton, and the hon. secretary, and after much work they recommended to the general committee that the plan of J. H. Taylor should be followed, and that the designing and construction should be carried out by Messrs James Carter and Co., under the direction of their architect, Mr. Smith. These recommendations were adopted. The work upon the new course was commenced in July last, and carried on, despite the weather, until November, when the job was completed. Speaking of the weather, it might be mentioned that the wet cost the Club directly over £400 in lost time and repeat work, to say nothing of loss of growing time to such seeds as were late sown. The design of the course had been most carefully considered. It was of such length as to satisfy the longest of hitters, but, at the same time, there were five really first-class short holes, and the length of all the others was so varied as to preclude monotony. No two greens were alike, and this was one of the features. The greens also were of ample size—large enough to hold even very wild approaches, but not so large that a man must use a brassie instead of a puttie ; and, from the management point of view, not so large as to become expensive in upkeep. Upon the completion of the actual construction the committee voted a further sum of money to be expended in the construction of bunkers through the green, and this money was mostly expended in erecting some main groups of bunkers which would greatly add to interest in playing, and would also serve as a nucleus for the further scheme of bunkering to be proceeded with at such time as more funds were available. It was to be regretted that there was not rather more contour in the land upon which the course was built, but steps had been taken to break up the flatness and to convert the whole into a wild heath. To this end some two thousand clumps of gorse and broom, and two hundred and forty trees of various kinds, had been planted between the holes, well away from the line of play. All these trees, &c., were the gift of Mr. Reginald Beale, one of the directors of Messrs Carter and Co., who, from the very first, had taken the keenest interest in the new course. At the conclusion of the work and its final passing as correct the Construction Committee handed it over to the Green Committee, and the latter reported that, considering the weather, the course was coming up well, and that already some of the greens were in excellent condition. Many times it had been asked : " When will the new course be opened ? " It was impossible to say. Everything depended upon the weather this Spring, and if all went well the opening might possibly be towards the end of June. It was proposed to utilise the existing barn and cow-pen, which stood upon what was known as the Charity land, to form the nucleus of a new Club house, and plans were being prepared with that end in view. As the question was a very important one, and the money to be expended fairly large, it was felt by the committee that great care would have to be given to the problem. The committee felt,

therefore, that they were unable at the moment to commit themselves to any definite plan. It would, of course, be very nice to erect straightway a Club house worthy of the course —not a great, ornate place, but one in keeping with the architecture of Stratford. This would involve more money, which meant more subscriptions to debentures. At the present moment these were not forthcoming, although he honestly believed that if interested parties would go and see for themselves what had been done there would be no need to ask. No report on the growth and construction of the new Club would be complete without reference to the help which had been received in time, brain, and money from certain individuals. There was no need to name these men, even if it were desirable to do so, but the Club was under a deep debt of gratitude to them for services rendered.

The report was adopted, on the motion of the CHAIRMAN, seconded by Sir WHITWORTH WALLIS.

Mr. WITHNALL, in proposing the re-election of Mr. Ludford Docker as President, said he recalled early days when they held meeting after meeting at which the present scheme was proposed, and at one period it looked as if the project would fall through. He had the temerity to approach Mr. Ludford Docker with a proposal which he could scarcely defend on business grounds, but he traded on the sporting spirit which was characteristic of that gentleman, and he responded to the bait and found the necessary money. He recalled also the anxious moments when the contract was pending, and when he heard of other birds hovering round seeking to pick up the worm. Mr. Docker was known to them as a gentleman of very high standing and a giant in the financial world, but what appealed to them was that he was a sportsman of the first water. They were proud to have him as their president.

Dr. BOX seconded the proposition, which was carried with acclamation.

Mr. DOCKER said it was not only a pleasure but a privilege to become their president for another year, and he could assure them that he would do his best for the Club.

On the motion of Mr. GEM, seconded by Mr. STILL, Messrs A. D. Flower, H. A. Jones, H. W. Bainbridge, and Captain A. R. West, R.N., were re-elected vice-presidents.

Dr. WELLS submitted the election of Mr. B. Norbury as captain. He was one of the original members who played when the course was at Wilmcote. He was a useful member, the best player in the Club, and a gentleman who had more time at his disposal than some of them. He (Dr. Wells) was loath to retire, and he hoped his resignation would be accepted in the spirit in which he made it.

Mr. POLLOCK seconded the motion, which was carried.

Mr. NORBURY thanked the members very much for his election, although he had hoped that Dr. Wells would go on for another year. It was just nineteen years since they elected him captain, and he should be pleased to act in that capacity for the new Club. His father was the first secretary of the old Club, and really started golf in Stratford. There were not many of the original members left. Mr. Willoughby Norbury, Mr. Lowndes, Mr. Park, and Mr. Bucknall, with one or two others, formed a club at Wilmcote, and that was how they came to live there. No sooner did they get there than another course was found at Stratford. He had heard it said that the new course would be uninteresting, but, personally, he did not agree with this view, as he thought the tee shots would be most fascinating. They would not be able to drive to the right or to the left, as on the old course, and get on the green with their second. Every shot would have to be placed. The greens were extraordinarily well bunkered, and it was marvellous to see what a transformation had been effected

42

since last September.

Mr. DOCKER said the members would desire to thank Dr. Wells for his services during the past year.

Mr. HILDER proposed the re-election of Mr. Knill as treasurer, and said they were extremely fortunate in having a gentleman of such high financial ability to discharge the duties.

Mr. WINTERTON, in seconding, said his brother banker and he were on the best possible terms, and he recognised the financial help which Mr. Knill had rendered in connection with the formation of the Company. They were greatly indebted to Mr. Knill and others for the aid given.

The motion was carried, and Mr. KNILL said it was a real pleasure to do what he could for the Club. It was delightful to know that the Club was going on so satisfactorily.

Mr. J. M. SMITH proposed the re-election of Mr. G. C. Evans as hon. secretary, and said they were very glad to welcome him there after the serious malady he had experienced. Another great struggle lay in front of him, and Mr. Evans had shown British pluck in expressing his willingness to undertake it. They were agreed that the Club was going to be the best in the Midlands, and they would try to make Mr. Evans' labours as easy as possible. When he (the speaker) was younger he had a certain weakness of character which, as he grew older, he largely overcame. His uncle used to say : " You know, my boy, a good-natured fellow is another name for a fool." Well, Mr. Evans was no fool so far as the Stratford Golf Club was concerned, and they could leave the business safely in his hands. He had not come there to praise or bury Cæsar, and he would say frankly that Mr. Evans was not always right. There were times when he (the speaker) had been in disagreement with him, and on those occasions he felt sure that Mr. Evans had been wrong—(laughter). There was one thing in which Mr. Evans had not varied—in his single-hearted devotion to the Golf Club.

Dr. BOX seconded the motion, which was agreed to.

Mr. EVANS thanked the meeting sincerely for re-electing him for another term. Although he differed from some of the committee at times, it was all in good part, and there was never anything personal in it. All had the interests of the Club at heart. He was deeply touched by the references made to his illness. He had to express to one gentleman thanks for more than he could ever repay. Not only did he give all his medical skill, but he gave him (the speaker) the moral courage to fight the illness, and it was that that saved his life. Other doctors came to see him, including Dr. Wells, with his cheerful face, that seemed to put the odds at 6 to 4 against one day, and 3 to 1 on another. Secondly, he should like to thank the Matron and the staff assistants, down to the probationers, for their kindness ; and, thirdly, the many people who made inquiries and sent gifts—from the working-people who used to meet his wife as she visited the hospital every day, to others who inquired over the 'phone and came by car. He did not realise that he had so many friends in and around Stratford.

Sir WHITWORTH WALLIS moved the re-election of Mr. Withnall as hon. auditor, and said they were very lucky in securing his services. He had done wonderful work in re-constructing the Club, and he piloted the Bill through the local House of Commons, the result of which was to be seen in the excellent balance-sheet which had been submitted.

Mr. EVANS, in seconding, said he shuddered to think what might have happened if Mr. Withnall had not been behind him. Probably he had been associated with Mr. Withnall more than anyone else, and his appreciation of that gentleman's services could not be over-estimated.

Mr. WITHNALL said he should be pleased to act as auditor, knowing that he had their confidence. He wished to depart from the mutual admiration business, and finish on a more serious note—that of finance. Further money would be required to put a coping-stone on their work as regarded the Club house, and they would want £1,000 to enable the committee to do what was thought to be necessary.

Dr. Wells, Messrs J. M. Smith, S. B. S. Walker, and G. Champ were chosen to serve on the committee, and the proceedings closed with a vote of thanks to the Chairman.

43

Mr G C Evans – Hon. Secretary at Welcombe for five and half years

Tiddington Road 1925–1994

Early Days

So in 1925 after 27 years at Welcombe Fields the Stratford-on-Avon Golf Club moved to its new course at Alveston Manor Farm. The new course over 6000 yards long had been laid out by J H Taylor, twice Open Champion, and constructed by James Carter & Co of Reading. A sum approaching £12000 had been spent on the course and club house, including purchase of the land, nearly 150 acres.

The situation of the course on the east side of Tiddington Road about ten minutes walk from Clopton Bridge, lies in a bend of the River Avon, a site selected by the early Britons two thousand years ago as a settlement. The sub soil was described as ideal. J H Taylor in his original report to the Committee stated "You can play 365 days in a year in slippers." Under the layer of rich light soil, a foot in depth, there is a deep bed of fine gravel with pockets of sand. It is undoubtedly one of the driest courses in the Midlands. The course generally is flat and originally was free of excessive timber and hedges.

The Club House

The club house quite unique, still retains its original unusual features, although it has been added to on a number of occasions. This eighteenth century barn and stables, conversion of which was incomplete when play commenced on the new course, has provided compact yet spacious club premises. The large club room reminds one of the baronial hall of some Elizabethan mansion with its massive fireplace and barrel ceiling. Here is the attractive "Nineteenth Hole".

The comfortable and well equipped wing for the ladies was originally separated from the main club room by an old world paved courtyard which formed a charming tea venue in summer. Ample parking space for cars was also provided from the start.

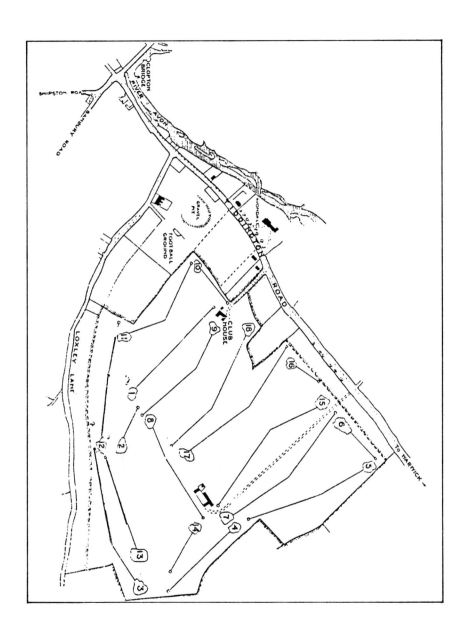

Plan of Course – Tiddington Road

46

The Club House at Tiddington Road in the 1930's

The old club house at Welcombe Fields was brought to Tiddington Road and erected for use as gentlemen's locker rooms, professional's shop, and caddie's shelter. Other buildings on the course consisted of a barn situated in the middle of the course which was later used as a workshop and store for the green staff and the machinery and equipment. Alongside this barn was a cottage and consideration was given to using it as a temporary club house and bar. Later thought was given to letting it at a rent not less than 6/- per week. This was deferred till the question of water supply could be settled. Sometime later it was let to one of the greens staff, Tom Ryman, who lived there and had seven children. (Was that surprising? There was no heat or lighting! – Author). Subsequently it was knocked down and the material used to build steward's quarters, adjacent to the club house. The hay crop on the course was sold to one of the members, Mr A G Newton for £138.

Play Commences

So play commenced on Saturday 29th August 1925.

An Extraordinary General Meeting of the Club took place on 7th November 1925 to consider increasing subscriptions for men to £6-2-0 from £5-5-0, and Ladies to £3-2-0 from £2-12-6, entrance fees similarly. It was agreed to plant 1000 trees along Loxley Lane boundary of the course.

Mr G C Evans who had resigned as Hon Secretary in May 1925 after five years, was presented with a grandfather clock, wrist watch and a silver cigarette box at the AGM held on 27th February 1926. Mr Brewster Norbury was re-elected Captain and by this date applications for debentures from members had been received for £5520.

The official opening ceremony for the course was postponed to allow the course to settle down, and during this period the caddies patrolled the fairways to remove stones.

On 1st May 1926 the first paid Secretary of the Club was appointed. Mr J S Andrew commenced at a salary of £100 per annum, on a three month trial. He was granted full membership and was entitled to lunch and tea when necessary. Purchase of office equipment was agreed at a cost not exceeding £10. In June 1926 a Steward and Stewardess were appointed at salaries of 25/- and 15/- per week.

On Sunday 1st March 1927 – the first "Hole in One" on the new course was scored by Mr J F Moore, father of Molly Moore, playing the sixth hole.

Roman Settlement

During the construction of the course evidence was discovered of the existence of an ancient Roman settlement, and so with the co-operation of the Committee further excavations were carried out, between 1925 and 1927, on the north side of the course, adjacent to the sixth tee. The remains of an ancient civilisation were unearthed, described conventionally as Roman or Romano British.

These excavations were conducted by Mr W J Fieldhouse CBE FSA of Austy Manor, Wooton Wawen, along with Mr F C Wellstood MA FSA and Mr T May MA FSA who took up his abode beside

The excavated Roman Settlement

the golf course to devote his whole attention to this work.

"The site comprised a tile kiln, water cistern washing tank or slurry hole, drying floor with hole and flues, ore roasting and iron smelting furnaces; lead smelting and de-silvering cupola; a number of ovens with fire holes and cupola, adjoining the north side of the golf links, near to the first milestone on the main Tiddington Road, and within the boundary of Stratford-upon-Avon and the parish of Alveston." A book on this work "A Romano British Industrial Settlement near Tiddington, Stratford-upon-Avon" was published in 1931, jointly by the Corporation of Stratford-upon-Avon and the Trustees of Shakespeare's Birthplace.

The Golf Club's First Steward

George Harris, professional at Welcombe Fields for 12 years had a non playing assistant, John Humphreys. When Harris had settled in at Tiddington Road, it was decided that he needed a "playing" assistant. So Humphreys was offered the post of Steward, and thus became the Club's first steward. Before being assistant to Harris at Welcombe Fields, Humphreys was a caddy. He was also a choir boy at Holy Trinity Church. His activity as a caddy often affected his attendance at evensong. One day Canon Melville caught him and said "Humphreys, if you are not at evensong this evening you need not come again." That was the end of John Humphrey's career as a choir boy.

John took up his work as steward; the stewardess being Ada Neal who lived in Snitterfield; and a "playing" assistant professional was engaged, Cameron Stuart. He did not stay long with the Club, leaving to go to America and was succeeded by Len Leach who remained with the Club for 36 years, replacing George Harris as professional when he died in 1929.

Mr Samuel Ryder

It was about this time 1925/26 that a certain Mr Samuel Ryder started to appear at Stratford-on-Avon Golf Club. He lived in

St Albans and was in the habit of bringing his daughter to Stratford for the theatre season, staying at the Shakespeare Hotel. During the day he would come into the Golf Club for refreshment and it was not long before he became a very great benefactor to the Club. He was elected an Honorary Member and whenever he came into the club house, John Humphreys (steward) would take him a tray with a bottle of Johnnie Walker whisky and a syphon of soda, compliments of the Club.

Samuel Ryder was the son of a Manchester seedsman, and having failed to persuade his father to sell flower seeds in penny packets, had moved south to St Albans to start his own business in Hertfordshire, where he made his fortune. There, later in life, to help recover from a breakdown, he took up the game of golf under the skilled and watchful eye of Abe Mitchell.

Following an unofficial match played at Wentworth in 1926, won by Britain with the massive margin of thirteen points to one, with one match halved, Mr Ryder presented a gold cup – The Ryder Cup – value £250 at that time, for competition between the professionals of America and Britain.

The first official match took place in 1927 at Worcester, Massachusetts, when the Americans captained by Walter Hagen beat the British team, captained by Ted Ray nine and a half to two and a half. The visit of the British team was financed by public subscription, a sum of £3000 being organised by "Golf Illustrated" to send a team of professionals to take part in the US Open Championship and also to play in the Ryder Cup match. Golf Illustrated subscribed £100 a sum matched by Mr Ryder himself and the Royal and Ancient Golf Club sent £50.

On 23rd March 1929 Mr Ryder was elected Captain of Stratford-on-Avon Golf Club, and in that year the British had their revenge at Moortown when the Americans, again captained by Walter Hagen, lost to the British captained by George Duncan, who in the singles beat Walter Hagen ten and eight.

To celebrate this victory by the British team, Mr Ryder gave a complimentary dinner to George Duncan and his team at the Shakespeare Hotel, Stratford-upon-Avon on Thursday 2nd October 1930.

Following these first two matches Mr Ryder passed his trophy

51

MONDAY, JUNE 7, 1926.

THE INTERNATIONAL MATCH.

GREAT BRITAIN'S SUCCESS AT WENTWORTH.

(FROM OUR GOLF CORRESPONDENT.)

The British professionals carried on in the Singles the good work begun in the Foursomes, and gained a smashing victory over their American brethren. It is perfectly true that the Americans are not yet acclimatized; also that they lacked several of their leading players, such as Sarazen, Farrell, Diegel, and Macdonald Smith. Still, when all is said, they had a fine side, and to trounce them thus was a proud feather in the caps of the British team. It ought to do British professional golf all the good in the world. In the last few years our players have suffered, and been encouraged to suffer, from an "inferiority complex." There should be no further excuse for this now. With their feet upon their native heath they should now, like Mr. Micawber, "stand erect before their fellow men."

The Wentworth course not only looked wonderfully pretty, but made an admirable battlefield, for it really is a fine, long, testing course, and it appeared to be in quite excellent order. The professionals made it look easy, which it is not, but they would do that for any course on a perfectly still day with a nice grey sky and greens slow and true. It ought to have suited the Americans very well, but it seemed to suit our men still better, for, with their tails well up after their sweeping victory in the Foursomes, they nearly all came in to luncheon with cheerful countenances and a pleasant little nest-egg in the matter of holes. In point of fact, they played collectively splendid golf, and the general opinion was well and trenchantly expressed by an American caddie—"Why is it that these fellows can play like a lot of world-beaters and then, when the Championship comes—their own Championship—they can't hit a balloon?" Well, on Saturday, at any rate, they could hit a balloon, for they outdrove and out-pitched their opponents, and I am disposed to think that they outputted them as well.

In a morning of much fine golf Mitchell's play stood out as a thing apart. He went round in 68, and that with the utmost ease and without having to do anything on the green except tap the ball dead from a few yards away. He was constantly putting for 3's at par 4 holes, and if he had had anything at all in the nature of a "day out" on the green Heaven alone knows what he might have done. Luckily, Nature does not waste her gifts and seldom allows the putts to go in on the day when all the iron shots are perching round the holes. Mitchell's score may be left to speak for itself :—

Out :—4, 4, 3, 4, 2, 4, 5, 4, 4)
Home :—4, 4, 3, 4, 4, 3, 5, 3, 4) 68

He holed one or two respectable putts, missed one or two short ones, and the rest was blameless, remorseless accuracy. He himself said that not for months had he played the shot up to the pin so well, and Barnes said that his adversary had been kind to him. Kind with a 68 ! What description could be more eloquent ? Mitchell bombarded an oak tree with his tee shot to the short eighth and, except for putting slips, I can think of nothing else to say about him. He made Barnes look comparatively commonplace and yet Barnes was round in 71 and playing a conspicuously courageous and resourceful game in which he was saving himself time and again near the hole. Havers

had a very fine round of 69—only one worse than Mitchell's—and was six up, but the highest scorer in point of holes was Gadd, who by sound, steady play and the avoidance of errors, piled up a lead of eight holes against Kirkwood. Kirkwood's play was quite too bad, to be true, and it seemed a pleasantly ironical circumstance that the man who can hit to left or right, high or low, apparently at will, and give such almost incredibly skilful juggling exhibitions with a golf ball, could not keep it out of the most obvious bunkers. Duncan always had the better of Hagen, who has clearly not yet got the " feel " of his game.

Of the Americans whom I had not before seen Melhorn looked very solid and sound, but I was more impressed by Watrous, a hard-looking, well-knit, wiry player with a neat yet forcible style who is a good putter in a manner clearly imitated from that of Hagen. It was very interesting to see T. D. Armour again. He was always a fine, slashing golfer when an amateur in this country, but his game has clearly gained much in solidity and he, too, has clearly studied putting to some purpose in a good school. He now hits the ball very pleasantly and smoothly on the green, with a suggestion, as I thought, of Mr. Ouimet in his style.

The afternoon was made exciting chiefly by another overwhelming exhibition by Mitchell and the ever-growing possibility of Britain winning the match with a completely clean sheet. Mitchell played the first six holes quite flawlessly in 23 shots, had a brief lapse, and took 6 to a long hole, where Barnes also came to grief, and then, presumably, he thought it time to begin. Perfect play for the next four holes would have been 3, 4, 4, 5. Mitchell did them in 2, 3, 3, 4, and that was enough for Barnes, who had struggled very gamely and well, without having that touch of luck on the greens which he needed so badly. One must resist a temptation to rhapsodize, but really Mitchell's golf was —. After him came a procession of victories, but at last there came a check, Melhorn getting the better of a hard finish with Compston and winning by a single hole. Last of all to finish were French and Ernest Whitcombe. French was dormy one, but took 3 to reach the home green. Whitcombe touched the hole with his long putt for 3, leaving French an 8-yard putt for the match. He missed it by the breadth of a piece of paper, having come home in 33.

The results were :—

SINGLES.

GREAT BRITAIN.		UNITED STATES.	
A. Mitchell, Private (St. Albans), 8 and 7	1	J. Barnes (unattached)	0
G. Duncan, Wentworth, 6 and 5	1	W. Hagen (Pasadena)	0
A. Boomer, St. Cloud (Paris), 2 and 1	1	T. D. Armour (Congressional)	0
A. Compston (Unattached)	0	W. Melhorn (Unattached), 1 hole	1
G. Gadd (Roehampton), 8 and 7	1	J. Kirkwood (Unattached)	0
E. Ray (Oxhey), 7 and 5	1	A. Watrous (Grand Rapids)	0
F. Robson (Cooden Beach), 5 and 4	1	C. Walker (Winterhaven, Florida)	0
A. G. Havers (Coombe Hill), 10 and 9	1	F. McLeod (Columbia)	0
E. R. Whitcombe (Meyrick Park), halved	0	E. French (Youngstown), halved	0
H. C. Jolly (Foxgrove), 3 and 2	1	J. Stein (Nashua)	0
Total	8	Total	1

FOURSOMES.

GREAT BRITAIN.		UNITED STATES.	
Mitchell and Duncan, 9 and 8	1	Barnes and Hagen	0
Boomer and Compston, 3 and 2	1	Armour and Kirkwood	0
Gadd and Havers, 3 and 2	1	Watrous and Melhorn	0
Ray and Robson, 3 and 2	1	McLeod and Walker	0
Whitcombe and Jolly, 2 and 1	1	French and Stien	0
Total	5	Total	0

Mr Samuel Ryder – Donor of the Ryder Cup
Photo: Molly Moore

53

SHAKESPEARE HOTEL
STRATFORD-ON-AVON

MENU

A Complimentary Dinner

given by SAMUEL RYDER, Esq., J.P.,

to

GEORGE DUNCAN

in appreciation of his successful Captaincy of the

Ryder Cup Team, 1929.

o o o

Les Huitre sur Neige.

—

La Tasse de Consomme Madrileine.

—

Les Solette Colbert.

—

Les Perdreaux au Mousserons.

—

Le Baron d'Agneaux a la Broche.

Les Pommes Biron.

Les Petit pois au Sucre.

—

Les Peches Melba.

Les Mignardises.

—

Les Canapes Diane.

Thursday, October 2nd, 1930.

54

Alex Herd

Toast List.

The King.

Abe. Mitchell.

E Ray

Our Host.

George Duncan.

The Chairman.

55

GOLF PERSONALITIES AT STRATFORD.

JUST A FEW APPROACH "SHOTS" WITH PEN AND INK OF THE INTERNATIONAL PROFESSIONAL GOLF FOURSOME AT STRATFORD -ON- AVON.

F.B. MOORE & J. SHIMELL ANDREW

"NIGGER"

"OFF WITH THE OLD SECRETARY AND ON WITH THE NEW!"

P.H. WELLS HAS TWO DISTINCT "ROUNDS" — ONE AS A GOLFER THE OTHER AS A DOCTOR!

ABE MITCHELL WORE GREEN STOCKINGS SO THAT WHEN HE WENT IN A BUNKER THE THOUGHTS OF GRASS ACCOMPANIED HIM!

SIR "ARCHIE" FLOWER, VICE. PRES. STRATFORD ON-AVON G.C.

Birmingham Gazette

TED RAY HOLDING A POST-MORTEM EXAMINATION OF A PUTT THAT STOPPED "DEAD" AT THE 7TH HOLE.

ANOTHER "12TH" WITH A "GROUSE" — THIS TIME NOT GLORIOUS! GEORGE DUNCAN SCOOPS FROM BUNKER TO BUNKER!

I SHOULD TRY A "SPOON" SIR!

ALEX HERD WENT ROUND IN 489 (69 STROKES AND 420 "WAGGLES")

IN THE EVENING A DINNER WAS "TEE-ED" UP IN HONOUR OF DUNCAN, THE BRITISH RYDER CUP CAPTAIN.

— NORMAN EDWARDS. —

3rd October 1930

NOTABLE GOLFERS AT STRATFORD.

PRAISE FOR THE LOCAL COURSE.

On Thursday of last week, at the Shakespeare Hotel, a complimentary dinner was given by Mr. Samuel Ryder to George Duncan in appreciation of his successful captaincy of the Ryder Cup team in 1920. Owing to ill-health Mr. Ryder was unable to be present, but at his request Mr. G. Muir presided, and he was supported by the Big Four (George Duncan, Abe Mitchell, Ted Ray, and Alex Herd), Sir Archie Flower, Dr. W. F. Box, Dr. P. H. Wells, Captain Banning, Messrs. R. W. Barrett, B. Norbury, N. Pollock, G. C. Evans, T. Noel Blagg, E. A. Barnard, S. Straw, A. T. Hilder, J. Shimell Andrew, E. B. Moore, and H. Leach. Apologies for non-attendance were announced from Mr. Ludford Docker, Mr. E. J. Hardy, Mr. W. E. Withnall, Mr. C. Pardoe, and Mr. Coventry.

The toast of "The King" was loyally honoured, following which Dr. Box proposed "Our Host," remarking that no man living had done so much for professional golf as Mr. Samuel Ryder. But for him the Whitcombe boys would not be in their present position. Mr. Ryder had been good enough to get George Duncan and his colleagues to come to Stratford and give an exhibition of their prowess on the course, and it was also at his invitation that the company had assembled that evening. Everyone was sorry that he was unable to be present, and wished him a speedy recovery—(hear, hear).

Mr. MUIR said he should report fully to Mr. Ryder the nice things that had been said about him, and he felt sure that the donor of the dinner would appreciate the kindly sentiments expressed.

Sir ARCHIE FLOWER asked to be allowed to add a personal expression of regret at the absence of Mr. Ryder. Those present would love to have had him with them, and he hoped that he would soon be able to join them again. Proceeding, Sir Archie said that that morning he received a letter from their host asking him to propose the important toast of " George Duncan," and he gladly acceded to the request. It was impossible to gild the lily. During the first nine holes that afternoon George Duncan had shown the spectators something of his true value, and he (the speaker) was fortunate in finding words—not his own—to foot the bill. Shakespeare, with his marvellous prophetic sight, wrote—

" This Duncan
Hath borne his faculties so meek, hath been
So clear in his great office, that his virtues
Will plead like angels, trumpet-tongued,
    against
The deep damnation of his taking-off."

Now, Mr. Ryder happened to live at St. Albans, the city from which Francis Bacon took his name when he was raised to the peerage. There were some deluded mortals who believed that Bacon wrote Shakespeare's plays, but Mr. Ryder was not one of them. Bacon was not born at St. Albans, but in London : he was not a sportsman, but a marvellous learned individual, fond of research. The only thing he discovered about golf was that the game was invented by the Irish and given to the Scotch, the reason for this being that if it had not been given it would never have got there at all—(laughter). It was extraordinarily interesting to follow matches of the sort played that day. The golf was wonderful. Take the very first hole. "Sandy's " drive was not a good one, and with the second he got no further than he (the speaker) would have done. Then " Sandy " played a beautiful shot, laying it within a yard of the pin, and one could imagine his partner saying, in the words of Shakespeare,

" With thy approach, I know, my comfort
    comes along."

But either Ray or Mitchell might be excused for exclaiming—

" By thy approach thou makest me most un-
    happy."

"Sandy" got his 4 all right. As they went along various vicissitudes were experienced. The greens were terribly unkind to "Sandy," who laid several putts just on the lip, and Shakespeare might have put into his mouth the words—

" Accursed be the hand that cut these fatal
    holes."

When they got to the tenth, and Ted Ray had an 18-inch putt and missed, he could not help feeling, on hearing Ted's murmur, that he was trying to improve on Shakespeare—(laughter). Scotland turned two up, but they were all square going to the eighteenth, which Scotland lost, and he (the speaker) could hear Shakespeare ask—

" Stands Scotland where it did ? "

and catch the reply—

" Alas, poor country !
Almost afraid to know itself. It cannot
Be called our mother, but our grave."

Was it not extraordinary how one found in Shakespeare lines that could be applied to every possible game ? Shakespeare was the great master of the English language, and those who played golf appreciated the value of language as a safety valve.

GEORGE DUNCAN said he scarcely knew why the dinner had been given in his honour. He was sorry that " the chief " was not present, and he was utterly at a loss to understand why the old country (meaning Great Britain and the North of Ireland) should discard such wonderful players as Aubrey Boomer and Percy Allis. " I may be one of those chosen to defend the cup," he continued, " and my opinion is that we cannot do without these boys. We have one or two good golfers in the making, but it will take two years before any of our young golfers will be able to beat an American who is an international player. I am not a pessimist, but I am going to predict that Great Britain will be beaten unless we have these men. Why should they be barred just because they are now associated with Continental clubs? We want to get a representative British-born eight, and we shall need our ablest. They have all sorts of rules in America, and they seem to make them as they go along. 'Where's there a will there's no sway'—(laughter)—and 'a little resistance is useful.'" Continuing, Duncan said that if he had been living in Shakespeare's day he should have hated to act as William's caddie, for a man with such eyebrows and forehead would never have got anywhere on a golf course. There were two reasons why champions were so good—one was that they had hearts of oak, and the other that their heads were of the same material—(laughter). It was nice to be back at the " Shak. "; back to the old course, which was improving. The greens were fast, and at the moment the fairways showed a luxuriant growth, though a mowing machine would work wonders. With a few visits from Abe, Ted, " Sandy," and himself it would be possible one day to produce a lady champion at Stratford-on-Avon.

TED RAY said it was the second occasion on which he had had the pleasure of playing on the Stratford course, which he characterised as a credit to the secretary and the members. It was up to the members to put their hands down and say, " We are going to have a course fit for anyone to play on." Although there was a distinct improvement since he played here for the first time, the lies were scarcely so good as they might be. He recommended that the approaches be cut anything from 10 to 15 yards back from the greens and tightened up to allow a really good approach, and have a certain amount of run to the pin. Referring to the remarks of Duncan, Ted Ray said the Americans had been very fair, inasmuch as they had said that they would play only American-born professionals against Great Britain in the Ryder Cup matches. He thought, therefore, that the P. G. A. were justified in saying that they should play only British-born professionals. Mr. Ryder had backed up professional golf splendidly, and if only they had here the backing that was forthcoming in America the old country would hold its own at any sport.

Sir ARCHIE FLOWER proposed the toast of the Club professional and the future Mrs. Leach.

Dr. WELLS submitted " The Chairman," and congratulated Mr. Muir on the admirable way in which he had deputised for the Captain of the Club, Mr. Samuel Ryder. They were proud of their Captain, he said, and hoped that he would continue in office for several years.

Mr. MUIR acknowledged the compliment.

In response to an invitation to say a few words, ALEX HERD said the course was playing very nicely indeed, and had improved a great deal since the last time he was at Stratford. He added that if the members kept trying, and did not listen to so many experts, it would improve still more.

At the close the company rose and sang " For he's a jolly good fellow," in honour of the donor of the feast.

Stratford Herald report
10th October 1930

59

Mr Samuel Ryder and the Ryder Cup Team leaving for the USA 1927

into the care of the Professional Golfers Association, via a Trust Deed. J H Taylor, James Braid and Joshua Taylor were witnesses to this historic document.

The growth of golf on the continent and the increasing prowess of continental professionals led to the team being extended in 1979 to embrace professionals from continental Europe.

There is no doubt that it is the ambition of every tournament professional to earn a place in the Ryder Cup team.

Great Golfers at Opening Matches on New Course, 1928

Although by this time Samuel Ryder had given up playing golf, his interest in the game was undiminished. He was instrumental in arranging a series of exhibition and challenge matches on the new course at Tiddington Road in the period 1927/30 including one for the official opening of the course on Friday 27th April 1928. The players who took part in these matches were all top line professionals of their time.

60

Abe Mitchell – fourth in the Open in 1920 – when it was won by George Duncan, who was 13 strokes behind Abe after 36 holes. Abe was in the final of the British Amateur Championship in 1912 when he lost to John Ball at Westward Ho.

George Duncan – British Open Champion in 1920, when the first prize was £100 and the total prize money was £225. George had a memorable Ryder Cup in 1929 when he won his singles, beating Walter Hagen ten and eight.

Arthur Havers – Winner of the British Open Championship in 1923. He was the last British winner for 11 years. He played in the 1927 Ryder Cup match at Worcester, Massachusetts when the British team was captained by Ted Ray.

Ted Ray – In 1920 at the age of 43, Ted won the US Open. He was the oldest winner. In 1927 he captained the British Ryder Cup team at Worcester, Massachusetts and at 50 was the oldest competitor in the Ryder Cup, until Ray Floyd played in 1993 aged 51.

Alex Herd – Alex won the British Open in 1902 and was second in 1920. He was the oldest winner on the British and European Tour, when in 1926 he won the News of the World Matchplay Championship at age 58. He was noted as the first "Waggler" of the club at address.

The Whitcombe brothers – Charles, Ernest and Reg. All played in the Ryder Cup, Charles and Ernest being paired together in the foursomes. Reg won the British Open in 1938.

Official Opening of the New Course

The official opening of the Tiddington Road course took place on Friday 27th April 1928 when the first of these matches arranged by Mr Ryder took place. Abe Mitchell and George Duncan beat Alex Herd and Ted Ray by three and two in a 36 hole four-ball match.

61

PROFESSIONAL GOLFERS AT STRATFORD.

A SUCCESSFUL GATHERING.

The new golf course was officially opened on Friday last, when four noted professionals—Mitchell, Duncan, Herd, and Ray—engaged in an exhibition four-ball match before a large number of spectators. There were speeches by the club's president (Mr. Ludford C. Docker), the Mayor (Councillor E. R. Thompson), Mr. S. Ryder (who brought down the professionals), and Mr. R. Y. T. Kendall (captain), the last-named gentleman asking Mr. Ryder to drive the first ball. As is customary on such occasions, a reward of £1 was offered to the caddie who recovered the ball and brought it back. Tipping (the tractor driver) was the fortunate finder.

When play was started a fresh south-easterly wind was blowing and the weather was beautifully fine. The recent dry spell had made the fairways hard and dry and the greens very keen. Accordingly, the ball, even for four such " professors," was difficult to control. The match was over 36 holes, Herd and Ray being pitted against Mitchell and Duncan. This was so formidable a task that Ray considered a three-hole start would be appropriate, a concession which, needless to say, was not forthcoming. As it turned out, his estimate was not far out; but had he and Herd not allowed their opponents to obtain a flying start there would have been little in it. As it was, Herd and Ray played the first five holes of the morning round badly and lost them all, and never afterwards were able to make up that leeway.

Of the play in general, it will be enough to say that all four great men played enough good golf to show how low scores are put together, and made enough slips to show that they, too, are human. To the spectator the difference in method of the four players was deeply interesting. There was Herd's string of purposeful waggles, Ray's splendid lurch, Duncan's grace and speed, and Mitchell's latent power and wonderful wrists and forearms—as much good golfing fare as anyone could reasonably digest in a day. After five bad holes, Herd and Ray played well. They were still five down at the turn, which was reached in a better-ball score of 35 and 39 respectively. Coming in, they won a hole back from Duncan and Mitchell, and went into luncheon four down, the full rounds being 68 and 73.

At the luncheon in the Club House between 30 and 40 guests were present, including the players and the captains and secretaries of various Midland clubs. The local captain (Mr. Kendall) occupied the chair, and extended a hearty welcome to the visitors. Major T. P. Cooke (of the Copt Heath Golf Club) responded.

After luncheon, Herd and Ray started well, and were only two down at the 21st hole, but, at the 27th, Duncan and Mitchell had regained their morning's lead. Coming in for the last time, the play of all was good, but after Mitchell and Duncan had closed the door at the 33rd hole, where they became dormy, Duncan banged it to and locked it at the 34th —the last short hole, where he got a fine two.

The respective second rounds were 67 and 68.

On Saturday E. Ray, A. Herd, and G. Duncan, together with Abe Mitchell, played a 36-holes exhibition match, the sides finishing all square. Mitchell and Ray were two up on Herd and Duncan at the end of the morning round, but the latter pair had squared the match at the ninth in the afternoon and a close homeward half also ended level.

On Friday Mr. W. F. Hutchings was the referee, and on Saturday Mr. G. C. Evans. Various members of the club acted as stewards. The arrangements, carried through under the direction of the secretary (Mr. J. Shimell Andrew) were very admirable, and the gathering proved very successful, some 500 people attending on Friday, and about 700 on Saturday. Many favourable comments were made on the course. A word of praise should be given to three young ladies—the Misses Phyllis and Mary Moore and Molly Seymour—and their companion who acted as fore caddies, armed with red, blue, and yellow flags. Thanks are also due to the following ladies who rendered assistance at the luncheon and in the refreshment tent : Mrs. Hilder, Mrs. Willan, Mrs. Park, Mrs. Boughton, Mrs. Andrew, Mrs. E. R. Thompson, Mrs. Hughes, Mrs. Ayrton, Miss D. Thompson, Miss Hastings, Miss Lucas, and Miss Seymour.

At the close of play on Saturday Mr. HARDY thanked Mr. Ryder and the professionals.

Mr. RYDER and Mr. ALEC HERD responded.

The prizes were distributed by Mrs. R. L. Hughes (captain of the ladies' section).

COMPLIMENTARY DINNER.

On Saturday evening a complimentary dinner was given by the Club to Mr. Ryder and the professionals, when the management of the Shakespeare Hotel placed an excellent menu before the members and their guests. There were several speeches, including an excellent oration by Alderman Flower. Vocal numbers by Messrs W. Gibbon, T. Birkett, and W. Court added to the pleasure of the evening. Mr. W. Court presided at the piano. Those present included the President, Mr. Ludford C. Docker (who occupied the chair), Mr. Samuel Ryder, Alderman A. D. Flower, Dr. Tweddell (amateur champion), Dr. Alexander, Dr. Box, Dr. Wells, Major Norbury, Prince Nasir Ali Khan of Jaora, Messrs Abe Mitchell, Alec Herd, George Duncan, Ted Ray, R. Y. T. Kendall (captain), E. J. Hardy, G. Muir, A. T. Hilder, B. Norbury, E. P. Gem, A. J. Knill, G. C. Evans, J. L. Docker, D. A. Marshall, W. Byrne, F. Hutchings, E. Barnard, R. L. Hughes, Spencer Walker, J. Shimell Andrew, T. Norbury, F. Guyver, F. Brooks, F. Tyler, S. H. Shakespeare, A. Lucas, A. C. Pauling, P. R. Giles, H. E. Sheldon, W. E. Withnall, and R. Bailey.

THE SPEECHES.

After the loyal toast had been honoured, Dr. TWEDDELL submitted " The Stratford-on-Avon Golf Club." With regard to the course, he said, he understood that three years ago it was merely a farm. If that were the case he thought the Stratford-on-Avon Golf Club was to be congratulated on the wonderful progress they had made. He played there last year with Mr. Perkins, and he must say that considerable strides had been made since that time. There was one thing about it—he thought it was rather too closely bunkered—(laughter)—but in any case it must be a good training ground. One could not play a loose second and get away with it. The Club were to be congratulated on their marvellous hospitality, and he thought it must be that hospitality, together with the beautiful surroundings and the old memories, that had drawn Mr. Ryder to Stratford-on-Avon. He understood that on his first visit he liked it so much that he was drawn to bring, first Abe Mitchell, and then four very famous players—(applause). It was a great privilege to any golf club to be supported in this way, and to have an opportunity of seeing the play of three ex-open champions and one of the greatest players in the world in Abe Mitchell—(applause). If he might just stray from the point a moment he should like to say they all hoped that this would be Abe Mitchell's year—(hear, hear). He had been knocking at the door for some years. He could play the shots all right, but had not had that little bit of luck that made all the difference. The speaker was sure he would win it this year, and he wished him the best of luck. Dr. Tweddell added that he was very pleased to be a member of the Club. He did not know a great many of the officers, but he must say they had a marvellous secretary—(hear, hear). He seemed to have arranged everything magnificently, and was dashing all over the place, doing everything as it should be done. He would hand over the toast to Dr. Alexander, and ask him to couple with it the name of the captain, Mr. Kendall.

Dr. ALEXANDER said when he was requested to play the second shot to Dr. Tweddell's tee shot he knew they would not want long speeches, so he would make it a short hole. Dr. Tweddell had reached the green, and all he had to do was to sink the putt. He had known the Stratford Club for some years on the old course. He came over from Broadway and had many a good game. He was very interested when they got the new course going, because he knew a great many of the members, and had had good games with them. They always liked the Stratford golfers to visit Broadway. "It is one of our regrets," added the speaker, "that our old Easter Monday match at Broadway has fallen through." They had a good game last Saturday, and Broadway was tremendously pleased that Stratford went down. He confessed that some of the leading Stratford players were otherwise engaged—backing losers at the racecourse—and so Broadway were able to take advantage of it and beat them. Dr. Alexander commented on the enterprise shown by the Stratford Club in getting that course, which was very good and promised to be better in the future, when the fairways had had time to make up and the general lie of the course had settled down. He thought it would then be a very fine course indeed. He was sure it would attract members and a great number of visitors. Stratford drew many people from the other side of the Atlantic, and now they had this golf course it would attract still more—(applause).

Mr. R. Y. T. KENDALL, replying, commented on the difficulty of his task, as he was neither an orator nor a golfer. Dr. Tweddell had said that the course was previously a farm. Not only was that so, but it was a very bad one ; a starved farm. It was extraordinary what had been done with the land in the time. If Dr. Tweddell found it too closely bunkered he wondered what was going to happen to his miserable foozles. He certainly found it more difficult than the average course, and it hurt one's self-esteem to do badly on one's own course. Mr. Kendall expressed regret that Broadway Golf Club did not go racing ; otherwise Stratford would never have had such a severe defeat as they suffered the other day. It was not part of his (the speaker's) job to give thanks to the friends who had been so kind as to promote that meeting. He felt, however, that the Club had had an extraordinary fillip during the last few days. He thought nothing could have done them so much good. It was difficult to get a new club well known, especially as local people were inclined to crab their own things—(hear, hear). It took America to discover what a fine fellow Shakespeare was, and that being so, in a non-golfing centre they needed all the outside enthusiasm they could get to show local people what a fine golf course they had. They had been a long time in realising it, and nothing would convince them better than the magnificent play they had seen on Friday and that day. Mr. Kendall announced that on the next day play for the record of the course would take place, and the Club had put up a purse of £25 for the winner. This he would hand to Mr. Ryder, with the request that he would award it the next day. He could not sit down without wishing their professional friends and their amateur friend the best of luck in the open championship. He hoped they would see a British victory, and pull it off against the Americans. To Mr. W. Gibbon, Mr. T. Birkett, and Mr. W. Court, Mr. Kendall tendered their very best thanks.

Mr. A. D. FLOWER, in proposing the toast of the evening, " Our Guests," said : " You who know me are aware that I have spent more of my time on theatre affairs than in playing golf, so you will understand if I use theatre, rather than golfing jargon in proposing this toast. In the world of the theatre the aim of a director is to get together a star cast, but if he is successful in doing so his troubles are not ended. Having got them together he has to allot their parts. He might have four good men who all want to play Hamlet, and then the fun begins ! To-night we have among our guests a man who has rightly earned for himself the reputation of being the great ' impresario ' of professional golfers, Mr. Samuel Ryder—(applause). He has undoubtedly brought to Stratford a star cast, and he has the satisfaction of knowing that he has got together four good sportsmen, and four good friends, who can be depended on to play their very best game. We are all very grateful to Mr. Ryder for his generosity and for what he has done for golf, and, as a native of Stratford, I would like to add one word more. He tells me that the air of Stratford suits him very well, so we hope that he will decide to take up permanent residence here. Now, what am I to say about the stars ? They have given us a wonderful exhibition of golf, and have made the game look so easy. Each in his particular way is a genius. Genius has been defined as 'an infinite capacity for taking pains.' How have they reached their exalted position as players to-day? Not by luck, but by hard work, by constant practice, by discipline, and by being blessed with the right temperament, for that is the only way in which a man or a woman can excel in any vocation in life. I am not going to attempt to gild the lily by dwelling on their individual merits. This afternoon we were told that George Duncan was not going to stay for this dinner. He is so modest that he did not like to wait to hear the flattering remarks that he felt sure would be made about him. It is one of the wonders of Shakespeare that he always appears to have written the appropriate word on every subject, even on Duncan's modesty. You will remember, in the play of 'Macbeth,' when Lady Macbeth is egging on her husband to kill Duncan—(laughter)—he says to his wife, 'This Duncan hath borne his faculties so meek.' I sat next to him through dinner, so I can vouch for Shakespeare's prophetic estimate of his character. But what subject did not Shakespeare know? He displayed an intimate knowledge of many and varied occupations, and books have been written to prove that the poet must have been a lawyer, a doctor, a gardener, or a sailor. I could show to you from his writings that he was a qualified veterinary surgeon—[A Voice: And a poacher] —certainly a fine sportsman. I am not going to claim that he was a golfer, but because of the terms he used it is apparent that he was familiar with the game. He had almost a prophetic vision of our new links when, in 'The Tempest,' he wrote of 'this short grassed green.' He makes use of the terms slicing, pulling, and to hook, but, like a true golfer, he does not recognise the term 'bogey.' As I walked round this afternoon, watching the international match, passages from Shakespeare kept coming into my head, and, curiously enough, several of these came from his Scotch play. I cut in as they started for the fifth hole, and saw Sandy Herd's ball find the bunker on the left, while the other three were up the middle. In imagination I heard Ray murmur to Mitchell, as they walked on together, 'What cannot you and I perform on the unguarded Duncan?'—(laughter). At the eleventh, when Mitchell put his second within eighteen inches of the pin, one of his Scotch opponents might well have said, 'By thy approach thou makest me most unhappy'—(laughter). When on several occasions the ball lipped the hole, but would not sink, the striker probably thought, if he did not say, 'Cursed be the hand that made these fatal holes'—(laughter). I have spent a good deal of time lately in trying to show people that a knowledge of Shakespeare enables one to do one's work better and to enjoy it more. The same argument applies to games. Believe me, the poet can be of real assistance to golfers. It is admitted that no one has ever excelled him in the command of the English language—(laughter). Let me give you just one simple example. Imagine yourself playing a match, and you hit, for you, a pretty good drive, but an unfriendly kick makes your ball finish in a bunker. You notice a grin come on to the face of your opponent's caddy as he mutters to your own, 'He's in it.' Think what a relief it would be to be able to turn on him and say, 'The devil damn thee black, thou cream faced loon.' If your opponent happened to be a parson, and pretended to be a bit shocked, what a satisfaction to be able to turn to him with a pleasant smile and tell him that you were simply quoting the master singer of the English language. If Shakespeare can do nothing else for golfers he can give them a plentiful supply of classic safety valves. I give you the toast of our guests. Long may they be 'in our flowing cups freshly remembered.'"

Mr. RYDER, replying, said it fell to his lot to be present at quite a number of functions of that character, but he did not think in all his experience he had ever had so much pleasure as that derived by coming to the ancient town of Stratford-on-Avon. "Your secretary," he added, "your committee, all the members of the Club, have been very kind to me, and have received me as though I am a very great man. Really I am not. My handicap at golf is questionable, but my interest in golf is above plus 25." Mr. Ryder said he had been trying to do what he could for the professional golfer, who, as a rule, had a very hard time. There were few plums in the professional ranks, and they were hard to find. It was a great pleasure to him to come in company with four great men—(hear, hear). They had four golfers there who had been famous in many a great match. His friends Mitchell and Duncan had travelled through America three times, and, as a rule, had beaten everyone they had met. Bobby Jones had been opposed to them on several occasions, but he had never beaten them. He ventured to say that if their friends had anything like luck in the next championship Bobby Jones would have to take a second, third, or even fourth place. He was much interested in the speech made by the gentleman who proposed the toast. It was one of the cleverest he had ever heard, and the apt quotations from Shakespeare were delightful. Mr. Ryder touched on one of the most serious things in the history of golf—the absence of good golfers coming along. It seemed, he said, that this was the spirit of the age. "The young men will not take the pains we had to when we were young. We had to work, to try, to study our business and profession if we were to succeed. But as soon as a young golfer goes round in 70 he thinks he is everybody."

When he asked himself who he should bring to Stratford to attract the crowds, the answer was, "Four of the veteran golfers"—(oh, no). "Yes," continued Mr. Ryder; "Abe's over 40, though I know he's like me and doesn't look it—(laughter). Now suppose we hadn't had these four veterans, where could you have got four young men to attract the wonderful attendances we have had?" They had three ex-champions and one promising young man who would be champion—(hear, hear). Abe Mitchell was the best player in the world, but he was stalked by ill-luck. It was gratifying to the golfing world that he had now got well and strong again after his terrible operation. "Of course," added Mr. Ryder, amid laughter, "I play with him frequently." It had been a great pleasure to him to meet them all, and to hear the delightful speech made by Mr. Flower.

Mr. E. RAY, on behalf of Abe Mitchell and himself, testified to their enjoyment of the visit. There had been a good deal of discussion about the numerous bunkers around the green. He understood that Stratford-on-Avon was very attractive to the American people, and they could take it from him that he thought they were justified, and were doing the right thing, in adequately guarding their greens. From a golf point of view he believed that he expressed his views across the water as regarded the construction of golf courses in England and America, and he thought there was a good deal of criticism in the English Press about the greens being guarded. He believed in thoroughly guarding greens. It made a man play for the pin, rather than the green, and he felt convinced that if they got their American friends there they would appreciate the well-guarded greens. Mr. Ray offered one or two little criticisms, including one on the bunker on the last green, adding, amid laughter, that he got into it that night with a very bad shot. He wished to thank the committee of the club for the way in which they had looked after them during their short stay in Stratford. He thought they had done everything in their power to make them feel comfortable, and he thanked them very much. He should also like to say one or two words about their friend Mr. Ryder, who was the professional's friend. He thought that in the last six or seven years he had done more for professional golf than, probably, anyone in the country—(applause).

Mr. ALEC HERD observed that when Mr. Ryder asked him to come along with those great golfers it gave him the greatest pleasure to accept. He was much interested in Mr. Flower's remarks on Shakespeare, although he did not think the poet was as good as Bobbie Burns—(laughter). He knew several of Burns' little poems, and he had a wonderful knowledge of human nature. Touching on the course, the speaker observed that it had been a very difficult ground of which to make a golf course. It was very, very flat. If they had got a little bit of hill and dale, and rises here and there, they could put up their greens and make them look a bit more spectacular. However, they had done the best they could, although the speaker suggested one or two alterations. The course would be a great asset to Stratford-on-Avon golfers. He was sure that in that day's golf they had seen an awful lot of bad shots and many good ones. He hoped they would benefit by watching the play of the champions and also of his friend, Abe Mitchell, who he hoped would win the championship this year—(applause). He thought Abe was one of the best golfers in the world—he would not say the best, because it was a difficult thing to determine. There was no one in the country who had a greater wish for his success in this championship than the speaker. They had other great players in George Duncan and Ted Ray. Ted was suffering from a bad arm, which he hoped would be better when the championship came round again. They were all delighted to hear of the great Hagen getting such a killing. The speaker had a round with Compston, who, he prophesied, would very nearly win the next championship. He was a great golfer and a good putter. He had enjoyed his trip, and hoped he would be able to come again with Mr. Ryder. " He is always challenging me to play matches," said Mr. Herd, " but I am always frightened to take them up. He is getting so good." Mr. Herd

described golf as the cleanest sport in the world. In all his career he had never known a dirty trick played by anyone in professional golf. He did not see many good professional golfers coming on, and that was a sad thing to say. It was not lessons their young golfers were wanting. They must have the ability and he will to get there, and spend much time in practice. Referring to the amateur champion (Dr. Tweddell) Mr. Herd said his was a very great performance, as it was a hard competition to get through. He wished Dr. Tweddell the best of luck, and hoped he would repeat his performance in many more years to come—(applause).

Mr. Docker, in a humorous speech, observed that Sandy had spoken quite a mouthful, and had told them all about the golf course. " He ought to," slyly added the speaker ; " he use more of it than I do "—(laughter). So he would leave out the golf course. They must have a course, and it must be guarded, because they never knew what these Americans would buy next—(laughter). He really thought that the great poet was also a golfer, because he liked his drink strong ; he objected to that light Flower's—(laughter)—and he could raise the elbow much better than Ted Ray—(laughter). They would never have any golfers in Stratford-on-Avon because they knew their Shakespeare too well. They had to have intelligence to understand Shakespeare but, as Sandy said, " Thank God for Bobby Burns." " Bobby once said—what did he say Sandy ?—(laughter)—'All's well that ends well,' or something like that ? No ! But he did say ' A man's a man for a' that ! ' " The speaker also thought his other words, " O wad some power the giftie gie us, to see oursels as others see us," might be useful to golfers. He touched on Mr. Ryder's services to professional golf and on Dr. Tweddell's magnificent performance, concluding by saying that he would beg another visit to Stratford-on-Avon.

Mr. HARDY, in submitting the toast of the President, said they could not conclude the evening without doing honour to Mr. Docker —(hear, hear). All the members knew what they owed to him for enabling them to carry out the scheme for the new golf course. They were all very poor people, and when the idea was mooted they had grave doubts as to how they could possibly acquire the land and lay it out in the manner they wished. Their president came to the rescue, and by his good offices they were able to make what they could claim to be a very good start, which would blossom at an early date into a success. Mr Hardy added that not only had the president done a lot in the early stages of the Club, but he was always at their right hand to give them assistance on every possible occasion. They felt deeply grateful for all he had done for them.

Mr. DOCKER, in reply, referred to the pleasure they had experienced in seeing such fine golf during the last two days. He thanked Mr. Hardy for the kind things he had said about him. Anything he could do he would be pleased to do if the opportunity offered.

The singing of the National Anthem concluded an enjoyable evening.

Stratford Herald report
4th May 1928

65

Mr Samuel Ryder playing the opening shot Friday 27th April 1928

Mitchell and Duncan were four up after the morning round and were still 4 up after the twenty seventh. They finally won on the thirty fourth green.

On 14th September 1928 Mr Ryder arranged for the fourth in a series of five 'Test' four-ball matches over 36 holes to take place at Tiddington Road between Abe Mitchell and George Duncan against Charles and Ernest Whitcombe. Then one year later he arranged an exhibition match for a prize of £100, on Saturday 14th September 1929, Abe Mitchell and Arthur Havers against the Whitcombe brothers. This game was played in glorious September weather. It was the first time that Mitchell and Havers had partnered each other as a side and they gained a notable victory beating the Whitcombe brothers by five and three over 36 holes. Mitchell was in brilliant form and with a score of 63 Mitchell and Havers were two up at the end of the morning round. In the afternoon Mitchell was again irresistible and won three more holes for his side, being splendidly backed by Havers. Mitchell went round in this four-ball in 66, beating his record for the course of 69, made the previous day.

One of the Flags carried by the Forecaddies 14th September 1929

Professional Golf Challenge Match

(By the courtesy of the Captain, Samuel Ryder, Esq.)

ABE MITCHELL

AND

GEORGE DUNCAN

VERSUS

C. A. WHITCOMBE

AND

E. R. WHITCOMBE

In the fourth of a series of five Test Four-Ball Matches (of 36 Holes),

— ON —

SATURDAY, SEPTEMBER 14th,

AT THE

Stratford-on-Avon Golf Club.

PREVIOUS RESULTS:

Match		Decided at		Winners
No. 1.	...	Verulum	...	WHITCOMBE BROS.
No. 2.	...	St. Andrews	...	MITCHELL & DUNCAN.
No. 3.	...	Verulum	...	MITCHELL & DUNCAN.

Play will start at 10.30 a.m. and 2.30 p.m.

TICKETS 2 6 each including free Car Park at the Club Park, if purchased prior to 12th instant.

LUNCHEONS (Stratford-on-Avon ¼ mile).

No Member's Car will be admitted to the Course except by a Pass.

EDWARD FOX & SON, PRINTERS, STRATFORD-UPON-AVON.

Notice of 4th Test Match, 14th September 1928

68

Acting as forecaddies in this match were Phyllis and Molly Moore, Molly Seymour and Lucy Whithall. They carried coloured flags, which later were autographed by Mr Ryder and the players and subsequently the autographs were embroidered. They have been carefully looked after by Molly Moore ever since.

On the next day Sunday 15th September 1929, the four visiting professionals played in four-ball matches with members in the morning, and in the afternoon Henry Longhurst, who later became a renowned golf correspondent and Television Commentator came to Tiddington Road and played in a match:

Henry Longhurst and Abe Mitchell
v
C Whitcombe and H Arnold (Midland Gold Medallist)

The same afternoon Arthur Havers and Eric Fiddian (ex Boys' Champion) were beaten by E Whitcombe and C Buckley (ex Aston Villa footballer).

On Thursday 2nd October 1930 another exhibition match took place between Ted Ray and Abe Mitchell v George Duncan and Alex Herd, which was followed by the previously mentioned complimentary dinner arranged by Mr Ryder at the Shakespeare Hotel, Stratford-upon-Avon, to celebrate the victory of the British team in the Ryder Cup match of 1929.

This series of exhibition matches was completed in 1931 when two top amateur golfers came to Tiddington Road, Dr Wm Tweddell, and T P Perkins.

Dr Wm Tweddell was British Amateur Champion in 1927, and Captain of the British Walker Cup Team of 1928 at Chicago Golf Club, and again in 1936 at Pine Valley. He was also a member of Stratford-on-Avon Golf Club.

T Phil Perkins was English Amateur Champion of 1927, and British Amateur Champion of 1928. He played in Dr Tweddell's Walker Cup team of 1928 at the Chicago Golf Club and was beaten by Bobby Jones 13 and 12, the biggest margin in the history of the Walker Cup. He also lost to Bobby Jones in the final of the American Amateur Championship of 1928 by ten and nine. This was the first time that the United States Champion had met the British Champion in the final.

Abe Mitchell playing from a bunker at the 16th hole, 27th April 1928

George Duncan. Abe Mitchell. Ted Ray.

Abe Mitchell. Mr G C Evens (holding flag). Sandy Herd. Ted Ray.
George Duncan

George Duncan finishing a drive
Photos: Molly Moore

Abe Mitchell following through – Ted Ray & George Duncan on the right

Mr Samuel Ryder watches the play on the 9th hole, 13th September 1929

Abe Mitchell. Arthur Havers. Charles Whitcombe. Ernest Whitcombe
Photos: Molly Moore

73

Arthur Havers

Molly Seymour. C Whitcombe, Phyllis Moore. E Whitcombe.
Molly Moore. A Havers
Photos: Molly Moore

Length of Course 5971 Yards.   Competition _Four--ball._   Standard Scratch Score, 75. Total Bogey, 76

Name of Player _Abe Mitchell_   Handicap_____ Strokes_____

Marker's Signature_____   Date _15ᵗʰ Sep 1929._

Marker's Score	Hole	Length yards	Bogey	Stroke Index	Score	Result
	1	407	5	7	4	
	2	166	3	17	3	
	3	399	5	3	4	
	4	379	4	11	4	
	5	398	5	5	4	
	6	132	3	15	2	
	7	448	5	9	5	
	8	367	4	1	4	
	9	379	5	13	4	
	T'ls	3,075	39		34	

Marker's Score	Hole	Length yards	Bogey	Stroke Index	Score	Result
	10	154	3	16	3	
	11	336	4	8	4	
	12	454	5	2	4	
	13	325	4	12	3	
	14	149	3	10	2	
	15	453	5	4	4	
	16	127	3	13	3	
	17	429	5	6	5	
	18	469	5	14	4	
	T'ls	2,896	37		32	

BOGEY PLAY

Holes won 1st half........... 2nd half............ Total.............

,,   lost   ,, ... ,, ... Total ....

Result

MEDAL PLAY

Gross Score 1st half 34 2nd half 32 Total 66

Less Handicap

Net Score

< THIS CARD MEASURES SIX INCHES THIS WAY >

Abe Mitchell's score card 15th September 1929

75

MIDLAND GOLF.

FAMOUS PROFESSIONALS AT STRATFORD.

FINE EXHIBITION IN FOUR BALL FOURSOMES.

The four-ball foursome is not the best form of golf. But it has its merits, which become apparent when it is played, as it was at Stratford-on-Avon on Saturday, by four first-class professionals. Mr. Samuel Ryder, captain of the club, was the provider of this golfing feast. He put up a prize of £100, and Abe Mitchell, the present Irish champion, Arthur Havers, the open-champion of 1923, and the brothers C. A. and E. R. Whitcombe, both winners of the " News of the World " tournament and many other important events, came to see that the money did not go abegging. So it was arranged, in order that the spectators should see as many strokes as possible, and that the players should not get their remuneration too lightly, that a 36 holes four-ball match should be played, Mitchell and Havers v. the Whitcombe brothers, and the crowd got their half-crown's worth. They saw an extraordinary number of very fine shots, and very few rank bad shots. Havers was responsible for the worst one of the day—his second to the first hole. His drive was a beauty, straight in the direction of the green, and then to the surprise of himself and of the onlookers he hit the next off the socket, and the ball darted out to the right. There were not many bad strokes, however, to encourage the spectators into believing they could have done no worse themselves; on the contrary, we can imagine many of them spoiling their own game by trying to imitate the shots of these four great men of the links.

To follow the day's golf was a treat, for it was glorious September weather, and the heat was tempered at times by a nice breeze. True, it was a dry, parched course over which we tramped, but the putting surfaces were absolutely true—witness the large number of properly hit putts that went down. The putting, indeed, was a notable feature in a day of excellent and consequently interesting golf. As might be expected from four prominent professionals, they played shot for shot up to the green with fine accuracy, and it was not until the greens were reached that fortune had much opportunity of showing her likes and dislikes.

Arriving at the Figures.

Mitchell and Havers were the winners by 5 and 3. They went in to lunch with a comfortable lead of two holes, still held it at the end of nine holes in the afternoon, and then proceeded to bring the match to a speedy close. In four-ball golf one's capacity for arithmetic is severely tested. It is all so bewildering, and those of us who were mixing duty with pleasure came to the conclusion that since the Mesopotamia there is no more blessed word in the English language than "approximated." But after much count and calculation, and assistance in that direction from the referee—Mr. F. B. Moose in the morning and Mr. Carl Bretherton in the afternoon—the following figures were arrived at: Mitchell and Havers (better ball), first round 63 (31 and 32); the brothers Whitcombe, 66 (33 and 33); second round, Mitchell and Havers (the full round was played), 66; the brothers Whitcombe 69. The standard scratch score of the course is 75.

There was not too much of the strong wind of strife about the contest. The players were out to win, no doubt, but the players were not keyed up as they will be, say, at Wentworth to-morrow, and quite a number of putts were conceded with the utmost generosity, as if a professional could not possibly miss a two-footer. Much detail is, therefore, not called for. If a selection had to be made one would choose Mitchell as the outstanding man of the brotherhood. From the tee he was the longest, and mostly the straightest, though with professional players of almost equal proficiency a difference of twenty yards on the tee shot makes no difference on the average course. Once only do we recollect one of the players taking wood for his second shot on Saturday. It was Mitchell's 3 at the fourth hole. That gave his side a lead—momentarily, as it happened—for at the next hole Ernest Whitcombe played a fine second out of a bunker and holed a stiff putt for a 3 to draw level. The sixth is a hole of 132 yards. Mitchell's tee shot was within a foot of the pin, but Ernest Whitcombe, who had been using his putter like a magic wand, this time ran down one of eight yards to secure a hard half.

Mitchell's Lucky Shot.

Havers put his side in front once more with a 4 at the seventh hole, and this time they clung to it. It was Mitchell's turn to sink an outrageously long putt on the eighth green, fifteen yards if it was an inch, and his side turned 2 up. They lost the eleventh to C. A. Whitcombe's fine 3, regained their two holes advantage at the next, and became 3 up at the thirteenth, somewhat luckily. It happened thus: Mitchell's approach was merry, and looked like over running the green, probably into the bunker beyond; instead, the ball was checked by the bank, began to trickle down the slope, and finished its course at the holeside—a 3. C. A. Whitcombe rammed down a ten-yard putt on the next green for a 2 and a win; he also took the next in 4, but a great 3 by Mitchell at the home hole once more put him 2 ahead.

This was a comfortable advantage with which to start the second round. This was played after lunch in a torrid heat, and was in the main free from adventure. The competitors got their figures without undue strain, and everybody was satisfied. Various fluctuations still left Mitchell and Havers with two holes in hand at the turn. A couple of halves opened the inward half, and then the fortunes of the match again began to swing the way of Mitchell and Havers. The 4 of the former at the twelfth, the second longest hole on the course, was good enough, so was the 3 of Havers at the next. The pair were 4 up, and they clinched matters by taking the fifteenth in 3, to win by 5 and 3. The players appreciated the services of four enthusiastic young ladies who acted as fore-caddies, tracked the ball with unerring accuracy, and waved the player towards it with a little flag. It was a valuable time-saving method.

T Phil Perkins. Dr Wm Tweddell
Photo: Molly Moore

On previous page: Birmingham Post report 16th September 1929

T Phil Perkins. Dr Wm Tweddell

T Phil Perkins. Dr Wm Tweddell
Photos: Molly Moore

Personalities of 1935

Although Perkins had played well in America, he had what was described as a "severe dose of the Bobby Jones's." Perkins later turned professional in the United States and was runner up to Gene Sarazen in the US Open of 1932.

At the AGM in April 1930 Mr J S Andrew retired as Secretary and was presented with a rose bowl and a cheque and then in 1935 he was elected a Life Member.

Mr Samuel Ryder was re-elected Captain in 1930 and became a Vice President of the Club at the AGM held in March 1931. He died in 1936 at the age of seventy seven.

Consolidation at Tiddington Road 1931–1939

The world recession and depression of the 1930s affected all walks of life, and Stratford-on-Avon Golf Club was no exception. Money was short and stringent control of expenditure was a feature of this period.

Estimates for the supply of hot water to the gents' and ladies' cloakroom were obtained in 1933. A figure of £31-17-0 was accepted – the cost to be spread over three years. In 1935 it was agreed that the ladies section be allowed 5/- per quarter for the use of the gas fire.

In February 1935 it was decided to fence the course along Loxley Road and land owned by Mr Pearce to allow sheep to graze on the course. An offer of £60-00 for twelve months' grazing was accepted from a Mr Cox, subject to all sheep being removed from the course for the Annual Open Meeting, any alliance or other meetings of societies.

In April 1935 there was a disturbance at the Club when the General Committee and Captain resigned en bloc in protest at the non election, at the AGM, to the Committee of the past Captain, Mr Sedgewick. It was felt that the Club had shown him great discourtesy. A special General Meeting of the Club was called and the Captain and Committee were re-elected along with the past Captain.

In June 1935 a sheep on the course was killed by a member's dog. It was decided that dogs would not be allowed in the club house and that dogs on the course must be on a leash.

To raise additional funds the Club issued invitations to local hotels to pay an annual fee and have permission for their guests to play on the course.

In the autumn of 1937 the General Committee agreed to increase the retainer of the professional, L Leach from £10-00 to £16-00 per annum. Permission was granted to ladies to use the Club lounge after 7-00 pm on Saturdays.

In January 1938 a tender of £24-2-6 for redecoration of the Club was accepted and the Secretary was instructed to obtain estimates for installing electric lighting and to ask Mr Spenser Flower if he was agreeable for money he had donated to the Club being used for this purpose. Tenders were obtained but it was decided not to proceed.

It was agreed to pay an additional 5/- per week to the assistant professional conditional on the professional contributing 2/6.

On 4th May 1938 the Committee accepted a gift of "The Captain's Tankard" from Mrs A V Johnson in memory of her late husband Dr A V Johnson. About the same time an anonymous donor presented a very beautiful clock for the ladies' lounge.

On 1st February the steward's wages were fixed at £2-14-6 per week with one day off, the Club to engage a relief for 5/- per week.

During 1939 the question of installing a watering system for the greens was given much thought. On 1st March £1000 was agreed for this purpose, but on 7th March the question of finance for this scheme was deferred. Further discussion took place on a subscription list for this scheme. It was agreed to put a list up in the club house as soon as a more accurate estimate was available, a Water Sub-Committee to decide when this list should be displayed, and a letter sent to members. By the beginning of May the sub-scription list stood at £290-1-6. Discussions continued throughout the summer on various options and by September agreement to go ahead was reached. On 9th September the scheme was deferred indefinitely, and in view of the national situation it was decided to return all subscriptions to donors with a letter of thanks.

During this summer of 1939 Stratford-on-Avon Golf Club won the Bainbridge Shield for the first time in its history –32 years. Our players were A E Winton Evans and A E Titchmarsh.

By now the war clouds which had been gathering were about to break and the world was to be turned upside down.

Second World War 1939–1945

The declaration of war on 3rd September 1939 had its immediate impact on the Club. John Humphreys (steward) and assistant professional (Fred Davis) had been called up to the Police War Reserve. On 6th September the matter of further payment of wages was deferred to the next meeting and Mrs Humphreys was engaged as full-time steward at 25/- per week.

L Leach (professional) had been called up with the Royal Artillery (TA). It was decided to pay his annual retainer of £16-00 immediately instead of in December and to inform him that his post would be kept open.

In December the Ladies' Committee was asked to do without the usual annual donation from the General Committee for the duration of the war. Discussion took place in March 1940 on the question of planting potatoes in the horsefield, but this was deferred and various small allotments allocated to members on the edge of the course for growing vegetables. Rents of 5/- to 10/- per annum were paid.

Gravel Extraction

In July an offer for gravel extraction between tenth tee and green was accepted at 1/3 per yard less ½d to ld way leave. A firm undertaking was given to leave the fall at three in one. The total gravel to be taken amounted to between £500 and £1000.

On 7th August 1940 permission was given for a small group of the Home Guard to drill on the course every Monday.

It was agreed that hens would be allowed on allotments only and a request from the Small Pig Keeping Council to form a small pig club was rejected.

Members serving in the forces were made Honorary Members for the duration of the War.

Conscientious objectors were not allowed in the club house or to use the course.

In the autumn of 1940 gravel extraction was extended to the first and 16th holes and 17th fairway.

On 17th March 1941 Warwickshire War Agricultural Committee inspected the course to see if it was suitable for ploughing for food production. It was decided that the only suitable part was the horsefield, at that time used as a sheep pen. Rather than await an order it was offered forthwith to a local farmer at a rent of £2-00 per annum. On 16th April Warwickshire War Agricultural Committee requested to plough the 12th fairway. This was agreed.

In mid-June, Mr Jacobs (Hon Greenkeeper) attended a Committee meeting to discuss the future of the course. A list was displayed asking for volunteers, Mr Jacobs to be in charge of the course and to control the volunteers. He reported that some members had already done good work and he nominated certain members to drive the tractor and others to tend the greens.

Royal Air Force at Stratford

By mid 1941 an initial training wing, No. 9 ITW of the Royal Air Force had been established in Stratford-upon-Avon. A green fee of 10/6 for two months, or for their period of training, was introduced for the RAF cadets. F/Lt L E G Ames, the Kent and England wicketkeeper/batsman, was elected an Honorary Member of the Club. Lockers for which rent had not been paid were collected and lent out to the RAF.

In July £1000 of mortgage was repaid and in September it was agreed that Lady members joining the services or the Land Army should be made Honorary Members for the duration of the War.

By November 1941 gravel sales had totalled 62394¾ yards at a sum of £4899-6-3 less tax £2146-15-0. A net figure of £2752-11-3.

On 3rd December Mr Jacobs was made an Honorary Member of the Club for the ensuing year in appreciation of his splendid work as Hon Greenkeeper. Mr Jacobs declined as he did not wish to give up certain privileges. On 7th January it was decided to recommend to the AGM that he be made a Life Member of the Club.

It was decided to remove the backs off the loose covers on the chairs in the lounge in order to repair the fronts, and on 7th January 1942 the Committee decided to ration sales of whisky – the Secretary to keep the supply in his office and to issue it if possible at the rate of one bottle per day.

At the end of the financial year the Company, for the first time in its history was in credit at the bank to the extent of £179-6-5. A sum of £2500 from the sale of gravel was transferred to a reserve account and the balance allocated to general funds.

On 7th October 1942 Squadron Leader L G Crawley, English Amateur Champion in 1931 and Walker Cup player was elected an Honorary Member. RAF cadets doing work on the course were granted temporary membership and were given drinks of tea after finishing their work.

A request by the Home Guard to requisition the cottage on the course was initially rejected but later agreement was reached for them to take over the cottage.

On 3rd February 1943 a request was received from Warwickshire War Agricultural Committee to plough up a plot, taking in the 7th, 15th and 17th fairways for the cultivation of foodstuffs. The Commanding Officer of 9 ITW offered to rent the land to be ploughed up for 30/- per acre for growing potatoes. An appeal was made by Mr Lea (grazing tenant) who was perturbed at the prospect of more land being ploughed. He was accompanied by the Hon Secretary, Treasurer, and S/Ldr Crawley, who gave details of RAF use and Home Guard activity. The War Agricultural Committee however persisted in its attitude and rejected the appeal.

In March 1943 a request from the RAF to use the 16th as a rifle range was turned down but it was agreed that it could be used for an assault course.

In April incidents of selling adulterated whisky in the bar resulted in the stewardess being discharged.

In November a momentous decision was reached after almost two years of discussion. The Committee decided to ban all dogs from the course and club house, the previous concession for members to have them on a lead being withdrawn.

Finance

Discussions had been taking place for some time in an attempt to buy out the original debenture holders and in November 1943 a scheme was finally agreed. Sir Martin Melvin and other friends of the Club had offered to provide sufficient finance to enable the Committee to pay 10/- in the £1 to all debenture holders. This was accepted at a meeting of debenture holders on 25th March 1944 in full discharge of debenture and accumulated interest. This decision of the Committee was approved at the AGM on 25th March 1944.

At that meeting a resolution was unanimously passed agreeing the action of the Committee in creating a new series of £250 debentures, limited to a total of £4000. Interest was 4½% and the subscribers had the right to appoint two of their members to act on the Committee and not to be subject to re-election. To accommodate these additional numbers the AGM passed a resolution authorising extension of the Committee from nine to eleven. At this same AGM of 25th March 1944 it was unanimously resolved that lady members should have the same rights and privileges as those enjoyed by the men and the right to vote at General Meetings.

By the autumn of 1944 £2500 of the new Debentures had been taken up by members.

By this time in the War, restricted supplies resulted in gin being rationed at the bar.

Wartime Organisation

Throughout the period of the War regular AGMs were held and Officials and Committee elected with the exception of a Captain. So for the duration of the War the Club functioned without a Captain.

1944 was the 50th Anniversary of the Club – the Club's Jubilee. To celebrate, it was decided to hold a nine hole match on 30th June 1944 between the Secretary's team and the Treasurer's team followed by a meal.

At the AGM on 24th March 1945 a hearty vote of thanks was accorded to Sir Martin Melvin for his gift of £750 debentures.

Some unrest now began to show itself and at this AGM a resolution was put – "That this meeting is of the opinion that the better interests of the Club would be served by the appointment of a male Honorary Secretary of the Club." An amendment that this should be left in the hands of the Committee was defeated and it was ruled by the Chairman that the proposition was carried without further vote.

There was also criticism of the work done on the course by the Hon Greenkeeper – Mr Jacobs. He resigned but withdrew his resignation and continued at the request of the Committee.

Difficulties were experienced at this time over the engagement of a steward and stewardess and some very unsatisfactory people were employed.

The War Ends

Following the allied invasion of Normandy in June 1944 and the rapid advance of the allied forces into the heartland of Germany in the spring of 1945, the War in Europe drew rapidly to an end. Germany capitulated and peace came in Europe in May followed by the finish of the War in the east in August 1945 when Japan surrendered.

The Immediate Post War Era 1945–1950

The war was now over and the Committee was able to start planning for a more normal Club existence. On 27th October 1945 a Club Manager was appointed. Mr A R Wheildon, who had retired after thirty one years as professional at Moseley Golf Club, became the Club Manager at a salary of £250-00 pa. Miss Phyliss Moore who had served the Club as Hon Secretary for five years was relieved of her post and was offered Honorary Membership, which she declined. At the AGM held on 30th March 1946 there were many expressions of appreciation of the services of Miss Moore.

It was now deemed appropriate to revert to the normal practice of electing a Captain and Mr A E Titchmarsh was unanimously elected.

Exhibition Match – Henry Cotton at Stratford

On 15th June 1946 a celebrity exhibition match took place. Mr Wheildon arranged for a match between Henry Cotton and Stanley Lunt versus Charles Stowe and Charles Ward – to play a four-ball game in the morning followed by a singles in the afternoon between Henry Cotton and Charles Ward. Stanley Lunt was English Amateur Champion in 1934 and Charles Stowe, once a miner, had lost in the final of the English Championship in 1937 and was a member of the victorious Walker Cup team in 1938. Henry Cotton at that time had twice won the Open Championship in 1934 and 1937, – he won again in 1948. Charles Ward was famous for being the first person to hole in one, twice, in the Open.

It was Henry Cotton's practice on these occasions to arrive in his Rolls Royce and change in his car rather than use the club house.

In the singles match Henry Cotton beat Charles Ward two and one.

During 1946 there was much discussion regarding improvements to the clubhouse. In particular the provision of electricity, heating in the locker rooms and water on the greens were the subject of much consideration. As a result it was decided to install electric light only and to proceed with water on the greens if a licence could be obtained. Funds were short and to meet the additional expense of these projects an EGM was held on 14th December 1946 at which it was agreed to increase subscriptions to £8-8-0 Gentlemen and £5-5-0 Ladies.

Those parts of the course under cultivation for growing food had not yet been released and in September 1947 a letter was received from Warwickshire War Agricultural Committee warning that they may have to plough up parts of the course again. On May 8th 1948 an order was received to graze sheep on the course. January 1949 saw steps being taken to reclaim the 12th hole. It was decided to plough, and then plant potatoes for 1949 and later seed it for 1950.

Morning and Afternoon Rounds

Celebrity Golf Exhibition

Souvenir Programme

1/-

STRATFORD-on-AVON GOLF COURSE

Saturday, June 15th, 1946.

Morning at 10.30—FOURBALL

HENRY COTTON and STANLEY LUNT

v

CHARLES STOWE and CHAS. H. WARD

Afternoon 2.30—SINGLES

HENRY COTTON v CHAS. H. WARD

Licensed Refreshments :: *Teas and Snacks*

MORNING FOURBALL

Yards	Hole No.	Scratch Score	Cotton	Lunt	Stowe	Ward
401	1	5				
166	2	3				
405	3	4				
410	4	5				
402	5	4				
180	6	3				
250	7	4				
118	8	3				
350	9	4				
469	10	5				
154	11	3				
355	12	4				
133	13	3				
330	14	4				
260	15	4				
102	16	3				
367	17	4				
379	18	4				
5231	OUT	69				

COTTON
LUNT
STOWE
WARD
IN

AFTERNOON SINGLES

Yards	Hole No.	Scratch Score	Cotton	Ward
401	1	5		
166	2	3		
405	3	4		
410	4	5		
402	5	4		
180	6	3		
250	7	4		
118	8	3		
350	9	4		
469	10	5		
154	11	3		
355	12	4		
133	13	3		
330	14	4		
260	15	4		
102	16	3		
367	17	4		
379	18	4		
5231		69		

OUT
IN
COTTON
WARD

Celebrity Golf Match 15th June 1946

The Fifties – Progress with Course and Amenities.

By the beginning of this decade the Club was firmly established at Tiddington Road. Five years had passed since the end of the Second World War, but there were still many restrictions and difficulties. It was a period when funds were short and constraint was very necessary. A number of measures were introduced to raise funds, including a Saturday night draw. Members were asked for gifts of tee plates, curtains, lockers etc. Despite the loss of revenue, sheep grazing on the course was abandoned, in order to improve the quality of the course. It was hoped to recover the loss of revenue by the sale of hay.

By 1952, showerbaths were being installed and investigations were going ahead into the provision of a new locker room. At the beginning of 1953 subscriptions were increased from £8-8-0 to £10-10-0 Men and £5-5-0 to £6-6-0 Ladies.

During this period there was much discussion on the question of the ladies having a vote at General Meetings. Following a resolution being made to deny the ladies a vote, which was then withdrawn at an EGM in March 1950, the matter was considered by a Sub-Committee. The outcome was that the Articles of Association were amended to regularise the position so that ladies were formally entitled to vote. These new Articles of Association were adopted at an EGM on 24th February 1951.

New Locker Room

At the AGM on 7th March 1953 members were asked to stand as nominees at the bank to raise funds to rebuild the locker rooms. Nine members came forward with offers of £100. This project was however turned down by the Ministry of Works. As a result a lesser plan was drawn up and work proceeded. A new professional's shop was built with help from Mr Pat Barrett and the old building converted into a drying room and additional locker space.

In 1953 Mr A R Wheildon was elected a Life Member and at the AGM on 6th February 1954 Mr Pat Barrett was elected to the Committee.

H Leach (Len). M J Busk
Photo: Jennifer Miramadi

91

In 1955 an appeal was made to members for funds which brought in £400. Various economies were made such as dispensing with a paid secretary and giving the catering to the steward. Subscriptions were raised to £12-2-0 Gents and £7-7-0 Ladies. In February 1956 David Thomas was elected Honorary Secretary.

The Club was asked to stage the 1956 Warwickshire Professional Championship and a County match against Somerset.

In 1957 a fund was raised to send the assistant professional M. J Busk to play in the Open Championship at St Andrews, in view of his fine performance in the Daks tournament.

In October David Thomas notified the Committee of his intention to finish as Hon Secretary at the year end. Steps were taken to appoint a paid Secretary and in December Mr W E Farmer was appointed at a salary of £100 per annum and £100 expenses. In the event David Thomas continued until May 1958 when Mr Farmer, now retired was able to take over.

At the AGM on 12th March 1958 David Thomas was elected a Life Member and Pat Barrett was elected Captain.

An increase in the number of members, more visitors and increased bar receipts, all contributed to an improving financial position as the decade came to a close.

During 1958 a new boiler and central heating were installed in the club house and considerable sums were spent on redecoration of the club house and locker rooms.

The Captain Mr Pat Barrett arranged for an exhibition match to be played by Harry Bradshaw and Christie O'Connor.

At the AGM on 7th March 1959 Mr Pat Barrett was re-elected Captain. He was thanked for his valuable help and tireless efforts on behalf of the Club and it was felt that the best interests of the Club would be served under his continued guidance.

A Building Fund was introduced to provide for future developments. Members were asked to subscribe to £10 interest free loans.

The Committee were recommending that a new ablution block be built. In addition the question of covering the forecourt was under consideration.

1959 was an outstanding year. There were a record number of visitors and green fees were a record at over £1000. The balance

David Thomas with the Town Bowl
Photo: Mrs N Thomas

93

STRATFORD GOLF CLUB'S 64 YEARS OF PROGRESS

By MAURICE WOODBINE

THE Stratford-upon-Avon Golf Club, one of the oldest in Warwickshire, was founded in June, 1894. It began as a nine-hole course on Wilmcote Moor some four miles north-west of the town.

The course was soon extended to include 18 holes, but the increasing popularity of the game brought about a search for suitable land nearer the town.

Three years after its formation, the club opened a ninehole course in Welcombe Fields, close to the Warwick Road. A subsoil of clay was an unfortunate feature of that choice but another 27 years elapsed before plans were begun for a move across the river to the present site on the east side of the Tiddington road.

Captained by Ryder

Mr. Samuel Ryder, who captained the club for two years, opened the new 18-hole course of 6,200 yards on April 27, 1928, one year after the series of professional matches between Great Britain and the U.S.A. for the cup given by him had started.

An exhibition match between four former Open champions— George Duncan, Ted Ray, Arthur Havers and Alex Herd— began the life of the club's present home, which was planned by another famous champion of the past, J. H. Taylor.

Beneath a foot depth of rich, light soil, is a deep bed of fine gravel with pockets of sand to provide the ingredients necessary for the construction of a course of high quality. The planting of fir, larch and beech, and the gorse and broom which already existed have helped to offset the flat nature of the links, which back on to a bend in the river.

Features of Course

The longest hole is the 12th (490 yards), where the fairway lies between spinneys. There are five short holes—the second (162 yards), the sixth (180 yards), the tenth (154 yards),

the 14th (200 yards) and the 16th (140 yards). These provide for a bogey outward half of 36 and a return of 37.

The pleasant clubhouse is a converted 18th-century barn and stables, providing a large clubroom in which the chief features are a massive fireplace and a barrel ceiling. An old-world paved courtyard is used as an attractive tea rendezvous when the vagaries of our summer weather permits.

A membership of more than 300 has been well served for more than 26 years by the professional and greenkeeper, H. W. Leech. His assistant for the past four years has been M. J. Busk, now 25, who has been well to the fore in Warwickshire events in recent years and will compete in most of this season's major professional tournaments.

Unusual Distinction

In 1944, A. R. Wheildon, who had then completed 31 years as professional to the Moseley club, joined the Stratford-upon-Avon club as manager and added the duties of secretary two years later.

Now enjoying his retirement at Shipston-on-Stour, Mr. Wheildon has the unusual distinction of having been engaged in every capacity concerned with golf clubs. He began as a caddie. Then followed employment as professional assistant, club and ball-maker, greenkeeper, professional course designer and steward.

For several years he was the Golf Correspondent of *The Birmingham Post*, and he has also broadcast upon the game.

94

The golf course at Stratford-upon-Avon, showing the fourteenth green with the old silo and barn in the background. *Below:* A tractor mower working on a fairway.

Birmingham Post
and Gazette article
15th April 1958

Left to right:
M J Busk. Harry Bradshaw. Pat Barrett. Peter Butler. Christy O'Connor.

Christy O'Connor driving 1958

sheet was satisfactory. The Building Fund had been well supported, by members making loans. In addition some members had made generous donations to the fund. It was decided to go ahead with the building of the new ablution block at a meeting held on 2nd March 1959.

The Sixties – The Course Transformed with Extensive Tree Planting

By the AGM held on 25th February 1960 members had subscribed a total of £2190 to the Building Fund, and at the end of the meeting a draw was held for the first subscribers to be repaid. The Club was able to repay a total of £1000 as a result of the improved financial position. This was another good year. Membership had increased and green fees were again a record. New equipment and tools were provided for the green staff and an improvement in the condition of the course was expected.

Group membership for RAF Gaydon and CAD Kineton was agreed for a fee of £30 pa. Three stewards and stewardesses left the Club.

Requests were received for the Warwickshire Professional Championship to be played at Stratford on 18th April 1961 and the Warwickshire Amateur Championship on 15th May.

Plans for a new dining room were drawn up during the autumn. In January 1961 plans for the new dining room were displayed in the club house. Tenders were received in March and the lowest accepted, from T Pettifer for £3037 (excluding lighting, heating and furniture).

1962 saw improvements carried out to the ladies' locker room. Tenders had been received and that from T Pettifer for £476 was accepted.

The greens had improved considerably following a programme of work recommended by outside consultants. Len Leach, professional, retired after thirty six years with the Club and was suceeded by Leslie Ball and in October Mr Andrew Tait was appointed Secretary in succession to Mr Farmer.

Subscriptions were increased in 1963 to £16-16-0 Gents and

1962 – C Wilkins. S Tyas (Captain). Eric Brown. J Larrad. Ken Bousfield. P Barrett. Max Faulkner.
Photo: Stan Tyas

£10-0-0 Ladies, to provide liquid funds for the purchase of new furniture, machinery and for a large tree planting programme.

By now the course was in very good condition, the greens particularly.

Mr Glover, President generously presented some carpets and furnishings to the Club.

A programme for planting trees on the course was introduced and started in 1963, and in January 1963 a very generous gift of trees was received from Redditch Golf Club. In October 1963 a sum of £150 was agreed for tree planting and a further £100 in September 1964.

During 1965 plans were drawn up to provide new buildings in the form of locker rooms, trolley store, kitchen and two flats for staff. A tender for this work was accepted from W A Cox (Evesham) Ltd for £23958. Much of the material was provided by knocking down an old Dutch barn and two cottages on the course. To finance these improvements a loan was accepted from the company operating the fruit machines of £8000, by way of advance rent on the machines installed in the club house. This was agreed on 6th December 1965. A further loan of £15000 was being negotiated with Warwick Building Society. Further finance was provided by raising subscriptions to £19-19-0 Gents and £12-12-0 Ladies at an EGM on 1st December 1965. On 10th January 1966 arrangements were made to rent a caravan as temporary living quarters for the steward until his flat was ready. A further £100 was agreed for tree planting.

In June 1966 the courtesy of the course was granted to John Humphreys in recognition of his long association with the Club.

Mrs H R Hughes was elected a Life Member in recognition of her long service to ladies' golf at Stratford, in the county of Warwick and internationally.

In September 1966 a County match was played at Stratford between Warwick and Somerset.

1967 was the year in which the Club introduced a Restricted Membership Scheme for 35 Gents and 15 Ladies; the International Match which has proved so popular was started by Laurie Dobson in his year as Captain. Also that year was unusual in that an outbreak of foot and mouth disease led to the possibility of the course having to be closed.

In 1968 Mrs Simpson, Life Member and Vice President had her 100th Birthday. The Committee marked the occasion by sending her a magnum of champagne. A further £150 was spent on tree planting.

During 1968–1969 there were many changes of steward and stewardess and in April 1969 Mr and Mrs Jillings were appointed as assistant steward and stewardess.

By this time the Club had a lengthy waiting list for new members.

Club Dinner 1966 – Left to right

Back Row: A Lambert. Tom Chadwick. J Busby. Ted Kerby. Cliff Veasey. Arthur Peart. Laurie Dobson. Wilf Rookes.

Front Row: Alan Bark. Pat Barrett. Ted Glover. Fred Kitchen (Captain). Charles Laverick

Photo: Margaret Chadwick

100

'International' golf match at Stratford

SATURDAY'S big contest on the Stratford course was, writes **A R J,** an international battle, and also internecine, and anyone forecasting a British victory was on safe ground—for once!

Club members were divided into national contingents, but with the preponderance of Englishmen, the other teams had perforce to be " diluted " by the inclusion of temporary acting Anglo-Scots, Anglo-Irish and Anglo-Welsh.

Each team played against two other sides over nine holes for each contest. At the half-way mark, cans of beer turned out to be booby traps for some players who opened them without precautions.

Following the match, a dinner was held at which the players, each wearing the appropriate emblem of his country, sat down to consume Scots broth, roast beef of England, Welsh rarebit, and Irish coffee.

Club captain and organiser of the event, Mr Laurie Dobson, then announced that England, with 10½ points, had won, closely followed by the Red Dragon contingent with 9, Scotland, with 6½ points, had just pipped the Emerald Isle. A cabaret entertainment rounded off a most enjoyable day.

Stratford Herald report 3rd November 1967

101

The Seventies – Big Improvements to Course and Premises. Increasing Financial Demands

The beginning of this decade saw a rapidly improving financial position and consequent continued development of the buildings; more tree planting, and the provision of automatic sprinklers on the greens.

In January 1970 Mr and Mrs Jillings were promoted to take over as chief steward and stewardess. They were very successful and well liked. Apart from a period of two years in 1972/74 when they tried a business venture of their own, they stayed with the Club until they moved to Bridgewater to be near their daughter in 1983.

In February Peter Rodgers and Mrs Burgess won the Warwickshire Alliance competition with a score of 64 net.

Mr R Robinson retired from the Committee after sixteen years as Captain, Competition Secretary, Green Chairman, and Vice Chairman of the Club. Mr C Wilkins also retired after the same period as Treasurer, Captain, and Chairman of Social Committee.

Subscriptions were increased at an EGM held on 5th December 1970 to Gents £25-00 and Ladies £16-00. At the same meeting expenditure of nearly £8000 was approved for the provision of automatic sprinklers on the greens plus approx £1000 for a new bore hole and pumping plant.

1971 proved to be exceptional financially with income exceeding expenditure by £7745 – a record. A Sub-Committee was formed to consider long term plans to provide additional accommodation for members and living quarters for outdoor staff.

During this year an interesting event took place when on 30th September a 'People to People' match was held with visitors from USA.

In 1972 the Warwickshire County Ladies Championship was held at Stratford on 2nd, 3rd and 4th May. By September plans for extending the ladies' locker room and lounge, and the Secretary's office had been drawn up. In October both stewards and their wives gave notice to leave and new staff, Mr and Mrs Davies took up appointment in November 1972.

In January 1973 the possibility of flooding the area of the gravel

1971 – Edmund Chaumeton (President) presents the Presidents Prize and Kendall Cup to Hassan Miramadi. Clive Morgan (Winner) holding the box Cup and Peter Rodgers (Captain) looks on

Photo: Jennifer Miramadi

pits in front of the sixteenth green was considered and a view was expressed that it could be done at little cost, but by February the idea was abandoned.

At the AGM held on 24th March 1973 it was reported that income had been static but expenditure had risen. All debts and mortgages had been cleared and the Club was in the "black". Stage one of development extension to Secretary's office and trolley shed had been started and the contract for the extension to the lounge and ladies' quarters would be signed in the next few days. Further development was envisaged in the form of building two flats to house green staff and other staff. More tree planting had been carried out. Mr and Mrs Davies had been dismissed because of stock losses and newly appointed steward and stewardess Mr and Mrs Evans had taken their place.

On 17th November 1973 an EGM was held to increase subscriptions to cope with higher wages, inflation, and alterations to the club house, lounge, ladies' quarters and professional's shop which were costing £16000.

INCOME AND EXPENDITURE ACCOUNT

£ 1970		£	£
	Course		
5753	Professional and Ground Staff...	6428	
1926	Upkeep of Course	1333	
31	Upkeep of Premises	156	
517	Rates and Water	529	
355	Lighting and Heating	404	
224	Printing and Stationery	289	
141	Telephone	137	
301	Insurance	328	
1241	Sundries...	1134	
61	Subscriptions	79	
10550			10817
	House		
2898	Wages	3129	
932	Sundries...	768	
404	Upkeep of Premises	64	
642	Repairs and Renewals: Equipment and Furnishings ...	487	
172	Rates and Water	176	
1065	Lighting and Heating	1213	
47	Periodicals	52	
6160			5889
	General		
744	Mortgage Interest	551	
14	Tithe	14	
777	Depreciation	1108	
5	Competitions	—	
42	Audit Fee	63	
116	Professional Charges	126	
1698			1862
18408			18568
2638	Excess of Income over Expenditure Transferred to Accumulated Fund		7745
£21046			£26313

Income and Expenditure account year ended 31st December 1971

GOLF CLUB LIMITED

FOR THE YEAR ENDED 31st DECEMBER, 1971

£ 1970								£	£
	Course								
1909	Subscriptions—Ladies ...	...	...	...	...	...	2462		
8542	—Gentlemen	...	...	...	...	...	10945		
217	—Juniors	...	...	...	...	...	220		
									13627
819	Entrance Fees ...	...	...	...	...	...	...		1602
273	Locker Rents ...	...	...	...	...	...	...		284
3864	Green Fees ...	...	...	...	...	...	...		5520
18	Sundry Receipts	...	...	...	...	...	...		18
15642									21051
	House								
3534	Bar – Gross Profit	...	...	...	...	...	...		3772
	General								
267	Bank Interest ...	...	...	...	...	...	...	203	
	Competitions ...	...	...	...	...	...	...	105	
1603	Profit on Dance, etc. ...	...	...	...	...	...	1182		
									1490
1870									
£21046									£26313

By the AGM of March 1974 Mr and Mrs Evans had gone and Mr and Mrs Jillings had returned as steward and stewardess. The buildings and extensions had been completed on schedule. Following a request for members to donate trees, more tree planting took place in early 1974. Two elms on the twelfth hole were treated for Dutch elm disease at a cost of £100 – with the possibility of bracing them at a later date at a further cost of £100. Later in 1974 plans for extensions to the kitchens were being considered at an estimated cost of £4000. Tenders for £3476 were accepted – work to start in November and be complete by mid January 1975. Additionally expenditure of £3500 was planned for new machinery. Consequently subscriptions were increased for 1975 to Gents £50-00 and Ladies £36-00 and again in 1976 to Gents £60-00 and Ladies £43-00.

During 1976 there was further discussion regarding a lake at the 16th hole. Creation of a 200 Club to raise finance for this project was put to members, but a poor response resulted in the matter being shelved at the AGM in March 1977.

During the early seventies a rapid spread of Dutch elm disease throughout the UK caused the loss of many trees on the course; along the sides of the third and fourth holes and the two large trees on the twelfth. Gifts from the ladies, the County Council and Mr Gittins of Shipston on Stour provided 2500 young trees which were planted on the course.

The high cost of the underfloor heating for the two flats brought about investigation into alternative systems.

In 1977 automatic sprinklers for the tees were approved at a cost of £3500 and arrangements were made to mark the Queen's Jubilee by holding an AM AM competition and in September another 'People to People' match was played against visitors from USA.

1978 marked the 50th anniversary of the opening of the Tiddington Road course and an AM AM was held on 29th April to celebrate this occasion. The author well remembers playing in this event – partnered by Tom Stewart (twice the Club Champion) and Mrs Joy Roberts, who had not been playing golf long, and was a little nervous at playing in Tom's company. She did very well and they had a very good score in the making, when a disaster happened to her. As she was leaving the 17th tee her trolley collapsed – she was very embarrassed – Tom picked up her bag and the author

Visitors from USA – 'People to People' September 1977

Photo: Jennifer Miramadi

Stratford-on-Avon Golf Club Ltd.

Golden Anniversary

of the

Official Opening

April 27th 1928

(The original inauguration was in 1894)

SPECIAL CLUB COMPETITION   AM - AM

TEES:— LADIES — LGU — MEN — WHITE

HANDICAP ALLOWANCE ¾

	H'CAP	STROKES	SIGNATURES	DATE 29-4-1978
PLAYER A				
PLAYER B				
PLAYER C				

HOLE	YARDAGE L.	M.	Gross Scores A	B	C	BEST NET.	HOLE	YARDAGE L.	M.	Gross Scores A	B	C	BEST NET
1	351	361					10	148	154				
2	151	168					11	344	367				
3	387	400					12	433	479				
4	334	421					13	321	355				
5	397	402					14	147	205				
6	131	181					15	454	476				
7	397	477					16	114	151				
8	312	363					17	415	476				
9	306	381					18	435	479				
TOTAL OUT 2766 3154 BEST BALL							TOTAL IN 2811 3142 BEST BALL						
							TOTAL OUT 2766 3154 BEST BALL						
												TOTAL	

Golden Anniversary 29th April 1978

108

carried the wheels and other bits. Joy was so upset that she duffed two shots on the approach and they missed winning the competition by one shot, finishing second to Violet Simpson, Don Lines and Jim Linham, who scored 62, winning the handsome silver salvers which they received from the Captain's wife, Mrs Sylvia Saunders. This occasion was also marked by inviting to the Club as many of the 1928 members as could be traced. Notices were placed in local newspapers and as a result fifteen ladies and gentlemen were entertained in the Club on the day of the AM AM 29th April 1978.

In November 1978 a new tractor and new Toro greencutter were purchased at a cost of £9500, and in July 1979 a tender was accepted from Ball Bros for £9302 to replace the oil fired central heating with gas.

In 1979 the 'Stags' (Seniors) was formed with their own competitions and matches with other clubs.

Modern Times – The Eighties and Nineties

This period was notable in the history of the Club; the greens had deteriorated badly and much hard work had to be carried out to restore them to a good playing condition. After much deliberation and experiment the trouble was diagnosed as thatch – thought to be the result of overwatering, through the over enthusiastic use of the automatic irrigation system. This trouble was being experienced at many golf clubs at this time and it seemed that the problem was the age of the course coupled with the use of modern watering equipment causing problems that only manifested themselves over many years.

Expensive equipment had to be purchased and hired to provide necessary treatment to overcome this problem and it was some years before satisfactory progress was made. Vertidraining, hollow tining, verticutting, slitting and dressing on a regular basis eventually restored the greens to a satisfactory condition. On a number of occasions consideration had been given to rebuilding and returfing the greens, but fortunately in the end this proved unnecessary.

This period was also marked by a number of changes in staff and alterations to club house and course.

Leslie Ball

110

During the summer of 1981 further excavations were carried out adjacent to and to the rear of the sixth tee, by Warwick Museum.

This year also saw the formation of the Society of Warwickshire Golf Captains in which the Club Captain 'Freddie' Walker played a leading role.

More tree planting took place in 1982. £500 was spent on trees planted to eventually screen the course from the new National Farmers Union building being erected at the rear of the sixth tee.

In August 1982, Leslie Ball, professional, announced his intention to retire after 21 years with the Club, and in December Pip Elson was appointed to succeed him, commencing on 1st April 1983.

During 1982 a fund was raised by contributions from members in memory of Mr Pat Barrett, which was used to purchase a special trophy to be played for annually on August Bank Holiday in the PB AM AM.

At the AGM in March 1983 Leslie Ball was elected a Life Member as a tribute to his long service as professional to the Club. In October Mr and Mrs Jillings retired after 14 years, as steward and stewardess, apart from a break of eighteen months between October 1972 and March 1974.

In 1984 the PGA Seniors Championship was held on the course from 17th – 20th May – prize money totalled £25000. Although this event took place early in the summer after a long and cold spring, the course was in reasonable order and the greens although still suffering the problems of thatch were presented in fair enough condition.

Improved conditions were created for the green staff at the barn, by the installation of electricity in the winter of 1985, telephone in 1988, and further improvements in subsequent years.

In April 1986, only two weeks after the author had been elected Captain, and the green staff had got the course looking very nice and tidy, a gale blew up and storm force winds of over 100 mph were recorded at Oxford. Eighteen trees were blown down on the course in the day and so the green staff had to buckle to, clear the fallen trees and tidy it all up again.

Two outstanding pleasant occurrences happened to the author during his year of office. The first was on 18th May when at his first major presentation he had the pleasure of presenting the Town

Bowl to the winner, his son in law, Steve Chaplin. The second was on 12th December when a very enjoyable occasion took place in the club house at the annual dinner. P B (Laddie) Lucas CBE DSO DFC was our guest speaker. He gave an enthralling talk not only about his golfing days as a Walker Cup player and captain, but also, when pressed to do so, about some of his exploits as a fighter pilot in World War II.

He told how on one occasion when on a sweep over Northern France he had his engine shot out by a ME 109. Laddie realised he had three options: bale out and be taken prisoner; ditch in the Channel and risk being picked up by the Royal Navy; try to glide back to the coast of Kent. He did not fancy the first two and so pointed the nose of his Spitfire at the club house on Princes Golf Club, where he was born. He managed to reach the coast with enough height to make a crash landing on the golf course. He then went on to say that "true to his golfing form he missed the first, fourth and fifth fairways and landed out of bounds in the marshes." This story bought the house down. But what a way to come home!

Annual Dinner 1986. Left to right.
John Gee DFC (Captain). P B (Laddie) Lucas CBE DSO DFC. Ted Kerby
(President). Dennis Whitehouse (Chairman) with the Ryder Cup
Photo: John Gee

Annual Dinner 1986. Left to Right:

A Dobbie.	P B (Laddie) Lucas.	Pip Elson
Runner UP Boys	Boys Champion 1933	Capt England Boys 1971
Cha'ship 1928	Walker Cup 1947	British Youths Ch'pion
	Walker Cup Capt. 1949	1971

Photo: John Gee

On the same night, the President, Ted Kerby had arranged for the Ryder Cup to be in the club house, the European team having won it at the Belfry, in the previous September, under the captaincy of Tony Jacklin.

During 1986/87 proposals to improve the gentlemen's locker and wash rooms were discussed and extensive plans to refurbish and upgrade them were put to the members. These were agreed and carried out at a cost of £26000, including extension of the Secretary's office and improvements to the hot water and heating systems. Following these improvements extensions to the dining room, entrance hall and spike bar were carried out at a cost of £100,000. These alterations were financed by loans from members, the brewery, bank overdraft and increased subscriptions. By the end of 1991 subscriptions had increased to Gents £315 and Ladies £245.

Captain 1993 – Francis Prentice.
(Chairman Centenary Committee)

'Captains All' – Past Captains Day June 1992. Left to right

Back Row: Gareth Hughes. Peter Clayton. Peter Miles. Peter Clarke. Peter Rodgers. Richard Ollis. Alan Saunders. Mike Gregg. David Moffat. Stan Thomas.

Front Row: John Gee. Hank Rushmere. Freddie Walker. Ted Marson. Ted Kerby. Alf Hanks. Laurie Dobson. Arthur Davies. Vic Burn. Bob Collett.

114

The completion of these additions and alterations to the club house has provided the members with facilities to meet the needs of the next phase of the Club's existence, whilst retaining the charm of its original buildings.

1992 saw the installation of a new irrigation system at a cost of £60000 financed by a levy on members. In addition changes to the 17th green and enlargement of other greens were carried out.

For 1993 subscriptions were increased to Gents £339 and Ladies £264, and membership totalled 770. Subscriptions were again increased at the EGM on Nov 27th 1993 to Gents £372, Ladies £289 for the Centenary year 1994.

It is 1994, the barrel roof bar is still the heart of the club house and is barely changed from its original form. There is no more cheerful and pleasant atmosphere to enter, than to go into the bar, on a cold winter day, after coming off the course, and to be welcomed by the roaring log fire. One feels confident that this is a feature that will be retained for the Club's next century.

The Ladies

Message from Mrs Bronwen Wyse – Ladies' Captain 1994

My years spent at such a prestigious golf club as Stratford-on-Avon have given me much pleasure. May I say how thrilled I am to be elected as Ladies' Captain in this our Centenary Year.

I am aware of the success of previous Captains and hope that I can maintain their high standards.

I wish the Club many more years of good, happy golf.

Bronwen Wyse

Throughout the hundred years of the Stratford-on-Avon Golf Club's existence the ladies have played a prominent part in its affairs.

At the inaugural meeting on 30th June 1894, three ladies were present.

As early as November 1894 a report appeared in the Stratford-upon-Avon Herald in which it was stated that Miss Agnes Crawford had won the opening Club competition at Wilmcote.

In the early years the Ladies' Section was always referred to as the "Ladies Golf Club".

Early Personalities at Welcombe Fields

By 1899 the Club had moved to Welcombe Fields. The first AGM of the Ladies' section was held on 8th April 1899 at which twelve

116

ladies were present. It was planned to hold mixed foursomes matches each month.

The first event was won by Miss Mabel Allfrey and the Rev O Mordaunt. The ladies had to find their partners, members of the Golf Club and the matches were played off a joint handicap, given by the ladies.

By 1901 the ladies had produced their first County player — Miss Mabel Allfrey being selected to play for Warwickshire against Middlesex.

The "Champion Cup" had been won by Miss Agnes Crawford, whose aggregate of three best scores was 302. She was technically the first Lady Club Champion.

By 1906 it had been decided to elect a Captain to help the Secretary with matches. Unfortunately records are incomplete and it is not known who this was. In this year Miss Agnes Crawford resigned as Secretary and her place was taken by Mrs Park who remained in office until 1920.

Miss Mabel Allfrey was elected Captain in 1908, by which time the ladies were organising regular medal and bogey competitions.

In 1913 the Club was officially affiliated to the Ladies Golf Union and a handicap system was introduced – previously a Handicap Committee had worked out its own.

In 1914 the Lowndes Cup for the bogey competition was donated by Mr G D Lowndes, Hon Secretary of the Club.

First World War 1914 – 1918

The First World War now intervened and the activities of the Ladies' Section were very restricted and no records exist of proceedings until 1920.

In that year an AGM was held and at the meeting it was decided that those who had qualified to play for the Monthly Bowl and Lowndes Cup in 1914 should be allowed to compete for them in April and May 1920. Miss Cicely Norbury was elected Captain and Mrs Hilder Secretary.

On 24th January 1920 a report appeared in the Stratford-upon-Avon Herald of the twenty third AGM of the Club. In the section

117

reporting the election of officers, Mrs Park is mentioned as being elected to the "Club" Committee.

Many alterations had taken place on the Welcombe course and in 1921 the par was changed to 74 and then back to 72. During 1921 and 1922 very hot and dry weather had produced drought conditions on the course, followed by very wet weather in 1923 which resulted in play being curtailed on a number of occasions. At that time teas were available at the Club – bread, butter and jam and tea, 9d.

Mrs C M Boughton was elected Captain in 1923 and again in 1924. This was the year that Mrs Simpson joined the Club. She remained a member for 45 years and lived to be one hundred and was elected a Life Member in 1955. She was known affectionately as "Ma" Simpson.

Mrs Simpson 'Ma'
Photo: Violet Simpson

Tiddington Road

The Club moved to Tiddington Road in 1925 and by 1926 first and second Team ladies' matches were being played in abundance – fifteen first and eight second had been arranged. Two Divisions were created for competition purposes – Junior (Handicap 26–36) and Senior (Scratch–25). These were later to become Bronze and Silver Divisions with slight changes to handicap qualifications. There were by now trophies for each division and fixture cards were on sale at 2d.

In 1927 Mrs Mildred Hughes was re-elected Captain for a third year and in this year the Club came third in the Warwickshire Championships and third Team matches were also introduced.

1928 was a quite momentous year – Mrs Hughes handed over the captaincy to Miss Phyllis Moore, but continued to play for the Warwickshire County first Team for a number of years, – Mrs (Archie) D Flower was elected President and Club Colours were introduced. "Blazers" best quality bound by beige and brown silk, to be worn by Silver Division only.' Later, this was relaxed, so that

STRATFORD-ON-AVON LADIES' GOLF CLUB.— In the Warwickshire ladies' county championship, played at Olton on Tuesday, the Stratford-on-Avon team secured third position. Thirteen teams competed, representing 10 clubs. Copt Heath won the cup for the third year in succession with a score of 265 ; Harborne were second with 280 ; and Stratford-on-Avon third with 282. The team comprised Mrs. B. Hughes 92, Miss P. Moore 93, Miss M. Seymour 97. Play was from the men's forward tees, and only gross scores were taken. In the afternoon Miss P. Moore tied for first place in the bogey competition. On the same day Olton sent an " A " team to Stratford. The result was as follows :—

STRATFORD-ON-AVON.		OLTON.	
Mrs. Hilder	1	Mrs. J. Marshall	0
Miss M. Moore	1	Mrs. F. Seins	0
Mrs. Spenser Flower	0	Mrs. J. Hartill	1
Miss J. Nelson	1	Miss K. Very	0
Mrs. Box	1	Mrs. F. Worrall	0
Mrs. Park	1	Mrs. H. S. Cooke	0
	5		1

Stratford Herald report 1927 – Warwickshire County Championships

STRATFORD-ON-AVON GOLF CLUB.

MONTHLY MEDAL COMPETITION.

P. R. Giles	84—15=69
E. G. Evans	85—15=70
S. B. S. Walker	81—10=71
S. H. Shakespeare	83—11=72
F. Naylor	95—20=75
L. C. Docker	92—17=75
A. D. Flower	90—15=75
T. Norbury	87—10=77
A. E. Amphlett	102—24=78
Dr. W. F. Box	97—18=79
T. W. Willans	91—12=79

* * *

RUNNING BOGEY COMPETITION.

Prince Nasir Ali Khan	18	3 up
Major Paul Norbury	8	2 up
Dr. Wells	3	1 up
T. Norbury	10	1 up
S. H. Shakespeare	11	1 up
Dr. W. F. Box	18	1 up
F. Sedgwick	16	1 down
W. F. Hutchings	4	2 down

* * *

LADIES v. MEN (FOURSOMES).

A foursomes match ladies v. men was played on Tuesday. The ladies were conceded nine strokes. Scores :—

LADIES.		MEN.	
Mrs. Hughes		Dr. P. H. Wells	
Miss Fyshe	0	Leech	1
Mrs. Hill		B. Norbury	
Miss M. Seymour	0	S. B. S. Walker	1
Mrs. Fyshe		P. R. Giles	
Mrs. Walker	1	E. Evans	0
Mrs. Simpson		G. Champ	
Miss M. Moore	1	R. Kendall	0
Mrs. Boughton		J. S. Andrew	
Mrs. Box	½	Harris	½
Mrs. B. Norbury		Dr. Box	
Mrs. Thompson	0	Mr. Potter	1
	2½		3½

* * *

MONTHLY BOGEY COMPETITION.

Played on Wednesday. Scores :—

Seniors :

Mrs. Simpson	4 down
Mrs. Hilder	6 down

Juniors :

Mrs. Jeffries	2 up
Mrs. Boughton	3 down
Mrs. Thompson	3 down
Mrs. Willans	5 down
Mrs. Newton	6 down

STRATFORD-ON-AVON GOLF CLUB.

APRIL RUNNING BOGEY COMPETITION.

Seniors.

Miss M. Seymour	all square
Mrs. Simpson	2 down
Miss P. Moore	4 down

Juniors.

Mrs. Thompson	1 down
Miss E. Seymour	2 down
Mrs. Willans	3 down
Miss M. Hastings	3 down
Mrs. Shakespeare	4 down

* * *

Playing at Finham Park on Monday, the local ladies sustained a heavy defeat. Scores :

STRATFORD-ON-AVON II.		FINHAM PARK II.	
Miss C. A. Norbury	0	Mrs. Glover (1 up)	1
Mrs. S. Flower	1	Mrs. Mills	0
Mrs. Willans	0	Mrs. Powell (7 & 6)	1
Mrs. Boughton	0	Mrs. Keeble (2 & 1)	1
Mrs. Park	0	Miss Gillit (1 up)	1
Mrs. Evans	0	Miss Sharpe (1 up)	1
	1		5

* * *

SPRING MEETING MEDAL COMPETITION.

Played on Tuesday. Scores :—

Seniors.

Miss P. Moore	90—13=77
Mrs. Simpson	98—19=79
Mrs. R. Hughes	87— 6=81
Miss M. Seymour	99—18=81
Miss M. Moore	100—19=81

Juniors.

Mrs. Ayrton	104—36=68
Mrs. Newton	101—26=75
Mrs. Willans	101—24=77
Miss Ballance	114—36=78
Mrs. Boughton	107—25=82
Mrs. Park	110—26=84
Mrs. Evans	114—29=85
Mrs. Thompson	121—36=85
Miss E. Seymour	118—29=89

* * *

GREENSOMES BOGEY COMPETITION.

Played on Tuesday. Scores :—

Mrs. S. Walker & Miss P. Moore	1 down
Mrs. Hughes & Mrs. Simpson	3 down
Mrs. A. D. Flower & Miss J. Nelson	4 down
Mrs. Willans and Mrs. Boughton	6 down
Mrs. Sheldon & Mrs. Thompson	10 down

Stratford Herald reports 1927 – Monthly Competitions

STRATFORD GOLF NOTES.

STRATFORD GOLF NOTES.

All golfers will rejoice at the achievement of Miss Phyllis Moore, the popular captain of the ladies' section of the Stratford-on-Avon Golf Club, who, when playing in a bogey competition in company with Mrs. A. T. Hilder on Monday afternoon, returned a card which showed that she was four up to bogey, and which created a new ladies' record for the course with a gross score of 78. This score is only six strokes more than the men's amateur record for the course, which was made by Dr. W. Tweddell, the well-known Stourbridge golfer.

Playing off a handicap of 7 she returned a net score of 71 and at the same time competed for the prize offered by the "Sunday Express" to any golfer who can complete an 18-hole round without recording a six. Succeeding up to the 18th, which has a bogey 5, she reached the green in three and her putt finished within a yard of the hole, but as luck would have it she failed to hole her next stroke, and took six.

The game was played under adverse conditions, insomuch that owing to the recent wet weather no advantage could be gained by "run." Playing the match on a Monday, the cutting of all the greens after the week-end growth had not been completed, and this made the pace vary considerably. Miss Moore's failure at the 18th is largely attributed to this cause. Her card read:—

Out: 4, 3, 4, 5, 5, 4, 5, 5, 5 = 40
In: 4, 3, 5, 4, 3, 5, 3, 5, 6, = 38

78

Local golfers will be gratified to learn that Mr. F. B. Moore, who is a brother of Miss Moore, has kindly consented to act as assistant hon. secretary to the Stratford Golf Club. Like his sister, he is an excellent golfer and plays off a handicap of 4.

The course at the present time is in remarkably good condition and is playing better than it has ever done. The fairways have improved tremendously with the favourable weather conditions, whilst the greens are equally as good as last year when Abe Mitchell described them as the best he had played on. All rough grass has been eliminated. Recently some American visitors described the course as an asset to Stratford-on-Avon.

To-day (Saturday) the usual Monthly Medal Competition will be competed for, whilst on Bank Holiday Monday there will be a men's stroke competition in the morning and mixed foursomes in the afternoon.

Arrangements have been completed for the club's annual open meeting to be held on September 25—27, when numerous cups and prizes will be competed for. The full programme will be published shortly.

Evesham Journal & Four Shires Advertiser – 2nd August 1930

all ladies were entitled to wear the Blazer – Silver Division to have a shield on the pocket.

During the years 1929–33 the ladies were asked to take the garden in hand and make it neat, and on the course were asked to use the men's sand-boxes (sand for teeing up). Boxes of a different pattern were being introduced for the men. Votes for ladies at General Meetings was a subject of discussion. Ladies were asked to contribute 2/6 each for dressing one fairway. Mrs Hilder resigned as Secretary and was honoured by gifts from the Club and the ladies. She was succeeded by Mrs Blagg. The ladies put forward a suggestion that bowling greens, croquet lawns and later tennis courts be constructed and that a lady (Hon Secretary) should serve on the House Committee.

A most unlikely happening, nowadays, occurred when a Ladies Medal was postponed to allow a society of 20 to play – to benefit the Club's finances.

1934 was the year in which Mrs Trixie Gould – a lady who was to figure prominently in the Club's affairs for many years – was elected to the Ladies Committee. A year later Mrs Prim Conway also joined the Committee.

1936 – The Ladies Begin to Make Their Mark

In 1936 the Sedgewick Cup was won outright by Miss Phyllis Moore and Stratford-on-Avon Ladies won the Warwickshire Team Championship at Moor Hall, on 28th April.

Second World War Approaches

In 1937 Miss Molly Moore, sister of Phyllis was elected Captain followed in 1938 by Mrs Simpson (Ma), who was to remain in office throughout the Second World War.

Shortly after the outbreak of war in September 1939 the LGU ceased to function and so the Ladies Section decided to have a Club Handicap System. All competitions were to continue except the Final Medal and Final Bogey.

WARWICKSHIRE LADIES' TITLE.

OPENING OF THE MEETING AT MOOR HALL.

THE TEAM EVENT WON BY STRATFORD-ON-AVON.

Warwickshire lady golfers mustered in force at Moor Hall yesterday when the team championship and the first round of the individual championship were decided. There was a record entry. The weather was favourable, the course in excellent condition and, thanks to the careful arrangements made by Mrs. Roderic Hughes, the honorary secretary, who had the assistance of Mrs. Jameson, ladies' honorary secretary at Moor Hall, a full programme was carried through with celerity.

Twenty teams competed for the county championship, which carries with it a cup presented by the late Mr. C. C. Chipman. Play was over eighteen holes, and each team was made up of four players, though only the three best scores counted. The course had been lengthened by 330 yards, making the total distance 6,292 yards, and as there was a strong breeze to counter at some of the holes it was not surprising that no competitor succeeded in reaching the par of 78.

The best round of the day was 81, returned by Mrs. Peppercorn, whose name has long occupied a prominent place in Midland ladies' golf. The feature of the round was accurate approach shots and a skilful use of the putter. Out in 40, Mrs. Peppercorn did the homeward half in one over par figures. The details were —

```
Out: 4 3 4 5 6 4 5 4 5—40
In   5 4 6 5 3 5 5 4 —41
```

Stratford-on-Avon "A" team took the cup with an aggregate of 270, and this despite the absence of their plus 2 player, Miss Phyllis Moore, who has met with a slight accident. Miss P. Simpson set the pace with 86, and Mrs. R. Hughes and Miss M. Moore kept within the early nineties. This was Stratford's first victory in the event. Harborne "A" finished only four behind the leaders, and Walmley and Copt Heath tied for third place. At one period Copt Heath appeared likely to make a close fight of it, but at the fourteenth Mrs. Challen played her opponent's ball and, as the error was not discovered in time, disqualification followed.

There were three tight finishes in the first round of the individual championship. Miss B. Bolt and Mrs. Chick claimed only a single hole advantage, but for sustained determination there was nothing to compare with the struggle

Birmingham Post report 26th April 1936

between Mrs. Nichol and Miss Fyshe, which went to the twenty-first green. The Leamington and County representative had a lead of one at the turn, and was two up with three to play. Miss Fyshe fought back pluckily, however, and when her opponent found a bunker at the last and took two to get out she seized the opportunity to square the match. Two extra holes were halved in 4, and at the next Mrs. Nicholls got the verdict with a fine 4, finishing up with a three-yard putt.

Miss B. Bolt took the Coronation medal, open to all members of Warwickshire clubs with L.G.U. handicaps, with a score of 87—9—78, which was the best nett. The best gross team prize went to Stratford-on-Avon, and for the best nett team prize Ladbrook Park and Sutton Coldfield "B" tied. The issue was decided on the last nine holes, and the honour went to Ladbrook Park.

To-day the second round of the individual event will be played over eighteen holes and the final to-morrow is over thirty-six holes. Details:—

TEAM CHAMPIONSHIP.

Stratford A.		Harborne "B."	
Miss P. Simpson	86	Miss Barman	93
Mrs. R. Hughes	91	Miss D'Abreu	95
Miss M. Moore	93	Miss Hale and Mrs. Le Couteur	102
	270		297
Harborne A.			
Miss Fyshe	88	Leamington and County B.	
Miss Line	93	Mrs. Renger	95
Miss Dawe	93	Mrs. Palmer	102
	274	Miss Moseley	111
Walmley.			308
Miss I. Pearn	87		
Mrs. B. Cooke	95	Sutton Coldfield "A."	
Mrs. Bacon	96	Mrs. Beastley	100
	278	Mrs. Russell	100
Copt Heath.		Miss Nott	102
Mrs. Peppercorn	81		302
Mrs. Rayner	98		
Mrs. O. Bird	99	Sutton Coldfield B.	
	278	Miss Joy	95
Leamington & County A.		Mrs. Weedon	104
Miss Nichol	89	Mrs. Rowley	104
Miss Ingest	95		303
Miss Kinsond			
	282	Stratford B.	
Ladbrook Park.		Miss J. Baser	99
Mrs. Bolt		Mrs. Simpson	102
Mrs. Harris	97	Miss V. Simpson	104
Mrs. Smith	99		305
	283	Hearsall A.	
Moor Hall A.		Mrs. Stroud	98
Miss Guthrie	95	Mrs. Trt	102
Mrs. Macaulay	97	Mrs. Holbrooke	105
Miss A. Freeman	97		305
	289	Olton B.	
Olton A.		Miss James	100
Miss Bentley	88	Miss Spittle	102
Miss Ort	96	Mrs. Heath and Mrs. Horton	105
Miss Harrell	105		307
	289		
Castle Bromwich.		Moor Hall B.	
Mrs. Chick	90	Mrs. Barry Morris	101
Mrs. Nicholson	99	Mrs. P. Hooley	109
Mrs. Ager	101	Mrs. Morgan	112
	290		323
Robin Hood.		Hearsall B.	
Mrs. Gummer	95	Mrs. Gray	103
Miss Yarwood	96	Miss Lynham	110
Miss Webb	105	Miss B. Simpson and Miss P. Balantyne	112
	296		325
Moor Hall C.			
Mrs. Carr	111		
Mrs. Garrett	111		
Mrs. J. Roberts	121		
	343		

GOLF

Stratford-on-Avon Golf Club monthly bogey competition resulted:

Silver Division

Miss M. Moore	4	3 down
Miss V. Simpson	13	5 down

Bronze Division

Mrs. Boughton...	22	all square
Miss G. Amos ...	36	1 down
Mrs. Chaumeton	19	3 down
Mrs. Norbury.....	24	3 down
Mrs. Workman...	19	5 down

* * *

Stratford-on-Avon Golf Club beat Leamington and County by two matches in a mixed foursome match at Stratford on Thursday week. Scores:

STRATFORD-ON-AVON.		LEAMINGTON.	
Miss P. Moore and H. Hardman	½	Miss Tanner and W. F. Wiseman	½
Miss M. Moore and Major Norbury	1	Miss Ringer and S. Wood	0
Mrs. R. Hughes and Rev. J. Sutton	0	Miss Rowland and G. Curle	1
Miss P. Simpson and H. N. Hopkins	0	Mrs. Craven and A. Butterworth	1
Mrs. Simpson and W. S. Wilson	1	Mrs. Lucas and S. Fellows	0
Mrs. Hardman and F. Workman	1	Mrs. Stephens and C. H. Palmer	0
Miss V. Simpson and Dr. M. Pembrey	0	Mrs. R. B. Palmer and H. Watson	1
Mrs. Gee and Dr. W. F. Box	1	Miss Z. Fellows and P. Wiseman	0
Mrs. Workman and G. R. Hookham	1	Mrs. C. H. Palmer and A. H. Green	0
	5½		3½

BOX CUP—FINAL

After a very good match Mr. P. G. Davidson (16) beat Mr. W. A. Robb (24) by 3 and 2 over 36 holes in the final of the Box Cup.

* * *

Stratford-on-Avon Golf Club ladies' open meeting medal competition on Wednesday resulted:

Silver Division.

Miss M. Moore.....	73—	4 =	69
Mrs. Smith..........	80—	9 =	71
Mrs. Coggins	82—	7 =	75
Miss Watson..........	92—16 =		76
Miss E. Pears........	78—	sc =	78
Miss Irving...........	87—	9 =	78
Mrs. G. Walker.....	94—16 =		78
Mrs. R. Hughes ...	84—	5 =	79
Miss P. Moore......	·79 pl 2 =		81
Mrs. Gould	85—	4 =	81
Mrs. Bishton..........	98—17 =		81
Mrs. Dowdall	98—17 =		81
Mrs. Duke...........	96—14 =		82

Bronze Division.

Miss Primrose........	93—22 =		71
Miss Taylor...........	94—19 =		75
Mrs. S. B. Walker	98—21 =		77
Mrs. P. Norbury ...	101—24 =		77
Mrs. Chaumeton....	97—19 =		78
Miss Ballance........	98—19 =		79
Mrs. Parsons.........	108—29 =		79
Miss Bennett..........	99—19 =		80

Stratford Herald report 17th September 1937

124

In June 1943 the Ladies' Committee was disbanded for the duration of the War. There were no minuted meetings between December 1941 and June 1943.

Mrs Boughton resigned and received a vote of thanks for her services to the Club over the previous eleven years.

The Post War Era

With the War over the ladies began to get back to normal and at an AGM held on 12th December 1945, with Mrs Spenser Flower in the chair Mrs Simpson was thanked for her long stint as Captain and Mrs Boughton as Secretary. She was succeeded by Mrs Gould. At the next AGM held in November 1946 it was decided to re-instate all competitions and there was discussion on an Open Mixed Foursomes competition.

In 1947 the ladies team won the Warwickshire Championship at Sutton Coldfield and the Warwickshire Foursomes at Copt Heath.

By the early fifties the Ladies' Section was firmly back on track and club matches totalling nine first Team and six second Team were being played each year. In 1950 an Australian Ladies Touring team was entertained.

Between 1954 and 1957 a difficult period was encountered when there was poor support for competitions and problems in raising teams for Club matches. Mrs Rene Greey however was made Captain of the County second Team in 1956 and her name was to feature prominently in County affairs in ensuing years.

In 1958 Mrs Mildred Hughes, who had for some time been very active in County golf matters, was elected Chairman of the International Selection Committee, and also on to the Council of the Ladies Golf Union.

Mrs Clare Workman who had been Captain in 1952/53 was again Captain in 1958/59 and during her last year the Club entertained a Commonwealth ladies touring team.

In 1960/62 Mrs Mary Bailey was Captain and by now the Ladies' Section was really flourishing. There were over one hundred members. A porch had been added to the ladies' locker room, provided in 1959 by money from the Spenser Flower Memorial

Fund. A very beautiful clock was presented to the ladies by Mr Dowdall, in memory of his wife. Very regrettably this was stolen from the club house in 1991.

In 1961 Mrs Greey won the recently introduced Midland Veterans Competition and the following year she was elected County Captain. By 1964/65 the section had grown to 173 members and the Club Championship was introduced in 1964, with a qualifying round and best 16 gross scores proceeding to a knock out: the final to be played over 18 holes. The first winner was Mrs Prim Conway, who for many years represented Stratford at both Club and County level. In 1965 a very successful Midland Championship was held at the Club. Mrs Greey was appointed to the Girls Championship Committee and was also made a Deputy Councillor on the LGU and ELGA.

Mrs Mildred Hughes was elected a Life Member of the Club in 1966.

Mrs J Peppercorn was Captain in 1967 and during the previous year she won both the Club and County Veterans trophies; she added the Club Championship in her year of office and also created a new course record. She was playing with Mrs P Luker and was doing a very good card, when a thunder storm developed. Despite the thunder and lightning Mrs Luker insisted that they carry on in the torrential rain and Mrs Peppercorn finished with a score of 74, her handicap was reduced from nine to four.

The Warwickshire Ladies County Golf Championship was once more held at Stratford and there was also a friendly match with Midland girls playing a Canadian girls touring team.

In 1968 Mrs Mary Bailey was again elected Captain and introduced an event which was to prove most popular – the Evening Mixed Foursomes. This competition, now played twice a year, has become probably the most popular social event of the calendar. Each year more people are wanting to play and the entry list is very quickly oversubscribed.

1969 saw the passing of Mrs Simpson, aged one hundred, who had been a member for 45 years and in whose memory her daughters later presented the Simpson Salver.

The Dowdall Cup was presented in 1970; for the winner of the newly introduced Past Captains competition.

STRATFORD-UPON-AVON GOLF CLUB

Duel: Round Charles for Hiley Bowl

LADIES' GOLF UNION SCRATCH SCORE 73

Date Aug 9 1967
Handicap 6

Player *Mrs. J. Peppercorn* Competition Strokes received

Marker's Score	Hole	Yards	S.S.S.	Stroke Index	Player's Score	Won+ Lost— Halved O	Marker's Score	Hole	Yards	S.S.S.	Stroke Index	Player's Score	Won+ Lost— Halved O
	1	355	4	5	4			10	154	3	14	3	
	2	162	3	17	3			11	355	4	2	4	
	3	405	5	9	5			12	440	5	8	5	
	4	350	4	3	4			13	330	4	12	4	
	5	402	4	1	5			14	145	3	16	3	
	6	160	3	15	3			15	455	5	4	5	
	7	394	5	7	5			16	121	3	18	2	
	8	337	4	11	5			17	415	5	10	5	
	9	319	4	13	4			18	450	5	6	5	
OUT		2884	36		38		IN		2865	37		36	

| | | | | | | | OUT | | 2884 | 36 | | 38 | |
| | | | | | | | TOTAL | | 5749 | 73 | | 74 | |

BOGEY PLAY
The score of every hole won or halved must be recorded

BOGEY RESULT

HOLES WON		UP	
HOLES LOST		DOWN	

HANDICAP   6

NET SCORE   68

BOGEY RESULT

Marker's Signature *Peggy Duka.*

Player's Signature *J. Peppercorn*

(1) To replace all divots.
(2) Smooth out footmarks, etc., in bunkers after play (use rakes where provided).

Joe Peppercorn's score card 9th August 1967

127

Ladies Captains Day 1968. Mrs Mary Bailey Ladies Captain
Photo: Violet Simpson

In 1971 Mrs Gould who had been the Ladies Secretary for many years and Captain in 1954/56 was made a Vice President of the Club and President of Warwickshire Ladies Veterans. She remained a familiar figure as she pedalled her "Sit up and Beg" bicycle across the course to the club house from her home in Loxley Road. Mrs E Chaumeton introduced a President's Prize Competition for the ladies.

1974 saw the introduction of an Invitation Day for the ladies and fifty members and fifty guests took part.

Mrs Eileen Evans had the distinction of captaining the County first Team in 1975, at the same time as she was Captain of the Ladies' Section. The same year Mrs Spenser Flower retired after 35 years as President of the Ladies' Section.

The Ferguson Brassie Competition was introduced by Mrs Rena Ferguson in 1977 during her year as Captain. This is a match between the Ladies Committee and the juniors, to give the juniors experience in Match play and guidance in etiquette. The same year the Club Championship was changed to 36 holes. The first contestants being Miss Anne Layton and Miss Eileen Hart – the match finished at the 38th – Anne being the winner. Mrs Boughton (Vice President) attained her hundredth birthday, and Mrs Eileen Evans won the County Veterans Championship, the fifth Stratford player to do so.

A special event was arranged in 1978 to celebrate 50 years at Tiddington Road. Fifteen people with memories of the opening were entertained by the Club and an AM AM Competition was won by a team including Miss Violet Simpson. The Stratford-upon-Avon Herald of 29th April 1978 carried a report of the day. Mrs V Comyn won the County Veterans Championship; Mrs Eleanor Walford received her County Second Team colours. Miss Linda Stewart was the winner of the nett competition in the Warwickshire County Girls Competition.

In 1979, one year after the Junior Girls Section of the Club had been formed, Miss Jackie Gregg won the Warwickshire Girls competition at the age of eleven.

Mrs Boughton passed her 50th year as a member, during which she had served as Secretary and Vice President: presented the Boughton Salvers, and had been elected as a Life Member. She died at the age of one hundred and two.

129

Golf enthusiasts remembered a day way back in 1928

REMINISCENCES flowed at Stratford Golf Club when the 50th anniversary of the opening of the course was celebrated.

The club entertained 15 people with memories of the opening in 1928 and there were many souvenirs to jog memories, on view. These included a complete copy of the "Herald", minute books, photographs and cartoons. Many of the exhibits were loaned by members past and present. Miss Mary Moore provided two forecaddy flags signed by Abe Mitchell and his brother, by Alec Heard, Ted Ray and George Duncan.

The guests at the 1928 opening went for tea in the club house and later took part in a putting competition. This was won by Mrs Prim Conway and she received a cup from Mrs L M Walker.

Stratford Golf Club was small in 1928 and it was only through the efforts of Mr Sam Ryder—whose name is known to golfers throughout the world—that many distinguished golfers of the day were persuaded to take part in the official opening ceremony.

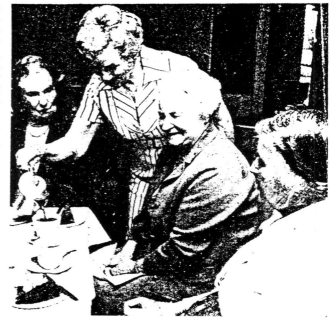

Above left: Mrs Gillian Walker pours tea for three people with memories of the day the course opened in 1928. They are: Mrs Mary Pardoe, Mrs Primrose Conway, and Mrs Trixie Gould. Mrs Gould is women's president of Stratford Golf Club. Above: A competition round of golf was won by a team of three which returned 62. The presentations were made by the club captain, Mr Alan Saunders, and his wife Sylvia (far right). The winning threesome was made up of, from left, Mr James Linham, Miss Violet Simpson, and Mr Donald Lines

SPECIAL CLUB COMPETITION AM - AM

TEES:— LADIES — LGU — MEN — WHITE

HANDICAP ALLOWANCE ¾

PLAYER	H'CAP	STROKES	SIGNATURES	DATE 29-4-1978
PLAYER A				
PLAYER B				
PLAYER C				

HOLE	YARDAGE L	M	Gross Scores A	B	C	BEST NET
1	351	361		4		3
2	151	168	4	3		3
3	387	400	4			3
4	334	421	4			3
5	397	402	5		3	4
6	131	181	3	4		2
7	397	477	5			4
8	312	363		4		4
9	306	381		4	4	3
TOTAL OUT	2766	3154			BEST BALL	24

HOLE	YARDAGE L	M	Gross Scores A	B	C	BEST NET
10	148	154			3	2
11	344	367			4	6
12	433	479	5		5	4
13	321	355				4
14	147	205	5			3
15	454	476	4		4	3
16	114	151	5			3
17	415	476			4	4
18	435	479	5			4
TOTAL IN	2811	3142			BEST BALL	33
TOTAL OUT	2766	3154			BEST BALL	29
					TOTAL	62

Winners score card 29th April 1978

On previous page: Stratford Herald report 5th May 1978

131

Golden Anniversary – Tiddington Road Course 29th April 1978
Left to right: Mrs Trixie Gould. Miss Mollie Moore. Mrs Cox.
Mrs Jill Bennett. Mrs Clara Workman. Mrs Mary Bailey.
Mr Cecil Wright. Mrs Margery Spink. Mr John Docker.
Mrs Bettty Barnard. Mrs Mary Pardoe. Mrs Primrose Conway
Photo: Violet Simpson

Another notable year was 1980. The new President was Miss Violet Simpson succeeding Mrs Trixie Gould, who retired after serving five years as President. Jackie Gregg again won the 18 hole Junior Girls Championship and her older sister Mandy played for the County in Junior Girl matches. Mrs Eleanor Walford was made County Second Team Captain.

This was the year when Mrs Mary Brook retired after fourteen years in office as Handicap Secretary – She had been Captain in 1971 and later became a Vice President.

In 1981 Mrs Chris Calverley and Mrs Gillian Gregg reached the final of the Dunhill Trophy Amateur Championship, and scored 37 points in the Stableford played at Woburn. Mrs Margaret Chadwick retired after serving ten years as Secretary of the Ladies' Section.

During the next few years a number of golfing successes took place. In 1983, Mrs Hilary Atkinson, a relative newcomer to the game, was awarded her County Second Team Colours and in the following season the Club reached the League semi-finals. 1984 saw the introduction of First Team Club badges and the first match against the Seniors (Gentlemen) followed by lunch. This event has continued twice a year and has proved to be very popular.

The Club won both the nett and gross competitions in the Inter-Club Warwickshire Team Championship in 1985 in Mrs Sheila Hansen's year as Captain but in the same year lost two of its stalwart members, both Vice Presidents, with the death of Mrs Mary Brook and Mrs Clare Workman. Mrs Prim Conway succeeded her sister as Ladies' President and Miss Mandy Newey was awarded her County Second Team colours. Meanwhile, Hilary Atkinson, having broken the course record that year, celebrated her captaincy the following season by winning the Club Championship, at the same time depriving Miss Sheelagh Murray of a hat-trick of titles.

In 1987, the same year in which Miss Pam Gibbs was playing in the Junior County Team, Mrs Ann Parry was awarded her County

Ladies Winning Team 1985
Left to right: Ann Parry, Hilary Atkinson, Mandy Newey, Violet Simpson, Sheila Hansen, Margaret Walford, Sheelagh Murray, Eleanor Walford.
Photo: Sheila Hansen

133

First Team Colours and took the Club Championship for the second year running.

Sadly, Mrs Iona Watson, who had been elected County President in 1988, died at the beginning of her year of office.

In 1989, Ann Parry was runner-up in the final of the Warwickshire Championship, losing to English International Miss Simone Morgan, who in the following year broke the Stratford-on-Avon course record.

In 1991, Mrs Hilary Atkinson was Captain of the County Second Team and during the second long hot summer in succession 74 handicaps were reduced.

At the AGM of the Club in 1991 an attempt was made to have the Articles of Association altered to allow ladies the opportunity to be elected onto the General Committee. The 65% support was

Ladies Past Captains Day – August 1993. Left to right:
Standing: Mary Watts. Hilary Atkinson. Ann Morgan. Eileen Evans.
              Mary Marson. Heidi Doherty. Sheila Hansen. Jennifer
              Miramadi. Anne Layton. Jeanne Holden. Olive Ladbroke.
              Anne Priest. Joan Glascoe. Val Comyn. Peggy Luker.
Sitting: Jean Hughes. Jo Peppercorn. Lillian Walker. Rena Ferguson.
              Violet Simpson. Peggy Styles. Joan Scott.
                        Photo: Ann Morgan

Prelude to the centenary. Left to right
Anne Priest (1890s), Pat Short (1920–30), Sheila Wissler (1940s),
Esme Blockley (1950s), Elizabeth Anderson (early 60s),
Marie Stewart (late 60s), Cynthia Straten (early 70s),
Pam Elliott (late 70s), Margaret Sheridan (80s),
Ileen Fisher (90s).
Photo: Anne Priest

insufficient, however, and the proposition failed. A second resolution the following year suffered a similar fate.

In 1992 in Mrs Heidi Doherty's year of office, during a very wet summer, the Ladies Champion was Mrs Pat Short who was also involved in a three way, twilight, sudden death play-off for the Birmingham Mail Midland Woman Champion of the year, taking third place. In the same year the British Senior Ladies Championship was held at the Club. Mrs Gillian Gregg was elected Captain of the County Second Team.

In this year the Club lost two more of its stalwart members with the death of two Vice Presidents, Mrs Mary Bailey and Mrs Margery Spinks, who had been associated with the Club since the early thirties.

1993 was a progressive year with a number of new innovations: A converted gross score system was introduced in February by

135

ELGA to speed up play in Stableford and Par competitions; Computerisation of the Ladies Handicap system was introduced; a library was started with the proceeds being sent to the charity "Talking Books for the Blind". Mandy Newey became the Ladies Champion beating Hilary Atkinson in the final. Violet Simpson became a Vice-President of the Club in March and Gwen Hazlett, one of the stalwarts, who had been Captain in 1963 died the same month. Many ladies represented the section in national competitions and the Captain Mrs Anne Priest and her partner Mrs Ileen Fisher represented the Club in the foursomes competition organised by the ELGA to celebrate their centenary. The Ladies Open Meeting had to be postponed in June as all the greens were flooded and was eventually played on a lovely September day.

The year came to an end with a Scramble Bring and Win competition followed by a supper, after which members were entertained with 'Prelude to the Centenary' – the 100 years' history of the Ladies' Section written in verse by Anne Priest (the Ladies Captain) and Pat Short, and performed by the Ladies Committee, wearing the golfing clothes of the appropriate decade.

Bridge

In addition to running the ladies' golf in a most efficient way the Ladies Committee has for many years organised regular bridge evenings and a series of bridge drives, in the Club, not only for the benefit of members but also to swell Club funds and raise money for charities. As early as 1910 bridge is mentioned in the minutes but more particularly from 1926.

PRELUDE TO THE CENTENARY
OF
STRATFORD ON AVON GOLF CLUB

**The History of the Ladies' Section – Written in verse by
Anne Priest and Pat Short**

One Hundred years ago in 1894
Stratford's first Golf Club opened its door.
This famous town – the Bard's home scene,
Now would be proud of its course so green.
The **Wilmcote Hills** was the first location
When three ladies joined in the celebration.

Then three years later, so the records say,
The **Welcombe Hills** was our course to play.
The ladies golfed, although just a few,
But over the years our Section grew.
Cups and trophies were given galore
For ladies achieving the very best score.

Now, with the help of the Committee so fair,
A little history I'd like to share.
What year and by whom were our cups given?
You don't know – Sit back and listen!

As you can see, when golf fashion began
Everyone looked like my old Gran.
Skirts long and straight, and shoes so tough,
Keeping feet dry, even in the rough.

With a handful of clubs and bag so small,
They played their golf for no prize at all.
*It was 32 years before cups got started
Mrs Wells gave the first – so kind-hearted.
The winners of **medals** throughout the year
To play in a **final** – best nett will clear.

In that year too, the best Bogey player
Was awarded a prize by a Stratford Mayor.
This time **Bogey** winners in a **Final** would play
E.Thompson's Cup, the reward on that day.

1925 saw our Club make a change,
New tees and bunkers to arrange.
The Club's new address was Tiddington Road,
J.H. Taylor the man where thanks are owed.
He designed the course on which we play,
Opened by **Sam Ryder** 3 years to the day.

Later in that year, 1928,
Mrs Flower gave cause to celebrate.
A greensome she thought would be fun,
We know it today as **Spenser Flower Greensome!!**

Another **Flower** – a **Lady**, no less,
Gave her **Cup**, a delight to possess.
So ornate, with replica too,
Qualifying Medal – it could be you.
Silver and Bronze, best eight of each,
Now played in Knockout – these Cups to reach.

As years went by so fashions moved,
And ladies in slacks no longer thought rude
War-time over with Victory in May
A silver box for the medal we play.
Club championship – the winner qualifies
And this **Victory Trophy** will be her prize.

The Cups keep a-coming – **Mrs Boughton** this time,
Gave Salvers so sweet – I wish they were mine.
'46 the year, 36-holes the task,
"Improve your Medal" was all she asked.
Never easy, as we all know,
Often it's the fittest that will show.

One year on, the hardest to win,
SUMMER KNOCKOUT, that's the thing.
Mrs Westwood's Cup, as we know it today,
Was the reward for consistent good play.

The Fifties saw fashion on the up,
No – this is not to rhyme with another cup!
But to show you that skirts had gone quite high,
Though we wouldn't dream of showing a thigh.

Coronation Year now, 1953,
A beautiful bowl for Gross Medals three,
Presented by **Dr Murray**, Sheelagh's Dad,
Displayed at home makes us proud and glad.

Two years on and **Miss Cowan's Cup** came,
To make us try harder at this terrible game!
Three nett Medals took the Cup home
The A.G.M. is when this winner's known.

A gap of ten years before the next Cup
For this it's golf skills and not just luck.
A Cup for **Club Champion, Mrs Wilson** gave,
Medal and Knockout – ALL efforts are made.

In 1966, only one year later,
A dear old lady – there's none greater,
Violet Simpson, whom we all know,
Thought **Vets** should have something to show.
So each year a Medal round they play
(If they'll admit age on that day!)
Violet's seen 28 win the Cup,
Hope you see many more – with luck.

The 60's saw change in the fashion scene,
Co-ordinates the thing – through the green.
Matching slacks and skirts, colours at last,
Dark grey and browns, a thing of the past.

Next, **Stratford's best gross** in the Open would win
A Salver of beauty – just the thing.
Presented by **Roderick** to remember his wife,
Mildred Hughes her name – golf was her life.

1970 saw two trophies to win,
The first presented by **Violet and Prim.**
This was a Knockout for handicaps high,
To make us play golf and really try!
The Simpson Salver was the one to appear,
How proud its winner is each year.
The second for Past Captains to win,
Mrs Dowdall's gift of a Cup so trim.

A dear Scots lady, there was no one keener,
Ex-Captain and President – her name of course, **Rena.**
Thought etiquette from Juniors should be here to stay
And ladies should encourage all forms of good play.
So a **Brassie** she gave from her Father's collection,
Played for yearly by a team from each Section.
Every Summer, from the 70's, a new disc can be seen,
Presented to the Captain of the winning team.

The 70's Miss Twiggy and bell-bottoms came,
And that showed itself in this golfing game.
Vizors too became something to wear,
To match your outfit – you must have flair.

The year was now 1974
Brother **Jennings** thought there should be more
He gave **Meg's Trophy** which was so fine
To play in Knockout through the Wintertime.

The **Engelbach's Cup** in 1979
Handicaps plus-30 alone may shine.
Tomorrow's Club champion could well be here.
Practice, just practice – then, maybe next year!

140

Now to the 80's and a popular man
Said "Through the year do the best you can
To reduce your handicap, that's very clear,
Not once, but the most, throughout the year."
Harry Brooks' Cup recalls **Mary,** so dear,
He loves to know the winner each year.

Clothes in this decade were in a whirl
As we all loved our own "Golf Girl".
Jennifer's designs spread worldwide
And we wore them with the greatest pride.

In '88 **John Newey** remembered **Sue,**
By giving a Cup, old silver, but new.
This time in the Open you must play,
Best Stratford nett will win the day.

Now into the 90's with colours aglow,
The Club saw it's very first Fashion Show.
We strutted and turned in Peter Anne clothes,
With a little applause our confidence grows.

The **Elliot's Trophy,** our newest prize,
Is made of china to delight the eyes.
You're as young as you feel – or so they say,
So a **Grandmother's** prize is on offer this day.

130 ladies – how our playing Section's grown
Since those early days when seeds were sown.
Sportsmanship and friendship is what it's about,
These can be found without a doubt.

That completes our trophies, when and what,
I wonder how many you all forgot?
So ladies, if you've still wine to pour,
I ask you – raise your glasses to 1994...

* Refers to trophies currently being played for in 1993

141

Ladies' Section

Presidents

1929–39	Lady Flower
1940–75	Mrs Spenser Flower
1976–80	Mrs T Gould
1981–85	Miss V Simpson
1986–88	Mrs P Conway
1989–91	Mrs R Ferguson
1992–	Mrs M Chadwick

1980	Mrs M Watts
1981	Mrs J Hughes
1982	Mrs J Scott
1983	Mrs M Watts
1984	Mrs J Holden
1985	Mrs S Hansen
1986	Mrs H Atkinson
1987	Mrs A Morgan
1988	Mrs J Glascoe
1989	Mrs J Miremadi
1990	Mrs M Marson
1991	Miss A Layton
1992	Mrs M Doherty
1993	Mrs A Priest
1994	Mrs B Wyse

Captains

1908	Miss M Allfrey
1912	Mrs Cowan
1920	Mrs Norbury
1923–24	Mrs Boughton
1925–27	Mrs M Hughes
1928–35	Miss P Moore
1936–37	Mrs Horn
1938	Miss M Moore
1939–41	Mrs Simpson
1946–49	Miss M Watkins
1950–51	Mrs Chaumeton
1952–53	Mrs C Workman
1954–56	Mrs T Gould
1957	Mrs M Jackson
1958–59	Mrs C Workman
1960–62	Mrs M Bailey
1963	Mrs G Hazlitt
1964–65	Mrs M Jennings
1966	Mrs P Luker
1967	Mrs J Peppercorn
1968	Mrs M Bailey
1969	Mrs P Styles
1970	Mrs L Taylor
1971	Mrs M Brook
1972	Miss V Simpson
1973	Mrs C Taylor
1974	Mrs M Kendall
1975	Mrs Eileen Evans
1976	Mrs O Ladbrooke
1977	Mrs R Ferguson
1978	Mrs L Walker
1979	Mrs V Comyn

Champions

1965	Mrs P Conway
1966	Mrs D E Greey
1967	Mrs J Peppercorn
1968	Mrs M Jackson
1969	Mrs J Peppercorn
1970	Miss A Layton
1971	Miss A Layton
1972	Mrs J Peppercorn
1973	Mrs P Conway
1974	Mrs P Blair
1975	Mrs I Watson
1976	Mrs E Walford
1977	Miss A Layton
1978	Mrs Eileen Evans
1979	Mrs E Walford
1980	Mrs H Atkinson
1981	Miss S Murray
1982	Mrs E Walford
1983	Mrs H Atkinson
1984	Miss S Murray
1985	Miss S Murray
1986	Mrs H Atkinson
1987	Mrs A Parry
1988	Mrs A Parry

1989	Mrs A Parry		1988	Sue Newey Trophy
1990	Mrs A Parry		1991	Grandmothers Trophy
1991	Miss S Murray			
1992	Mrs P Short			
1993	Miss M Newey			

Trophies

Hon Secretaries
Year Elected

1928	Flower Cups
1928	Spenser Flower Greensomes
1946	Boughton Salvers
1946	Victory Trophy
1947	Westwood Cup
1953	Coronation Bowl
1955	Cowan Cup
1961	Veterans Trophy
1964	Club Championship
1969	Mildred Hughes Trophy
1970	Simpson Salver
1974	Meg Jennings Cup
1979	Thirties Cup
1988	Mary Brook Trophy

1898	Miss A Crawford
1906	Mrs Park
1931	Mrs Hilder
1932	Mrs Blagg
1933	Mrs Hilder
1945	Mrs T Gould
1953	Mrs P Conway
1956	Mrs T Gould
1963	Mrs Tombs
1967	Mrs E Evans
1968	Mrs A Cartwright
1971	Mrs M Chadwick
1981	Mrs B Clifton
1986	Mrs A Priest
1989	Mrs D Jeffries
1992	Mrs I Fisher

Top Scorecard

Length of Course 5,253 Yards.   Competition Michelin Bogey   Scratch Score, 75. Bogey, 75.

Name of Player Phyllis Moore   Handicap 4   Strokes

Marker's Signature .... Date 17/8/32

Hole	Length yards	Bogey	Stroke Index	Score	Result	Hole	Length yards	Bogey	Stroke Index	Score	Result
1	130	5	7	4		10	130	3	16	4	
2	151	3	17	4		11	298	4	8	6	
3	335	4	3	5		12	410	5	2	4	
4	434	5	11	4		13	272	4	12	4	
5	385	5	5	4		14	131	3	10	4	
6	129	3	15	2		15	409	5	4	4	
7	394	5	9	4		16	110	3	18	3	
8	304	4	1	4		17	386	5	6	5	
9	319	4	13	4		18	396	5	14	4	
T'ls	2,711	38		35		T'ls	2,542	37		38	

BOGEY PLAY.

Holes won 1st half..... 2nd...Total......   Gross Score 1st half 35 2nd 38 Total 73

" lost " ......, ...Total......   Less Handicap 4

Dorothy Blagg Hon Sec -   Net Score 69

Bottom Scorecard

Length of Course 5,253 Yards.   Competition ....   Scratch Score, 75. Bogey, 75.

Name of Player Phyllis Moore   Handicap 4   Strokes

Marker's Signature .... Date July 9th 1934

Hole	Length yards	Bogey	Stroke Index	Score	Result	Hole	Length yards	Bogey	Stroke Index	Score	Result
1	130	5	7	4		10	130	3	16	3	
2	151	3	17	4		11	298	4	8	4	
3	335	4	3	4		12	410	5	2	5	
4	434	5	11	4		13	272	4	12	4	
5	385	5	5	4		14	131	3	10	3	
6	129	3	15	3		15	409	5	4	4	
7	394	5	9	5		16	110	3	18	3	
8	304	4	1	4		17	386	5	6	4	
9	319	4	13	5		18	396	5	14	5	
T'ls	2,711	38		37		T'ls	2,542	37		35	

BOGEY PLAY.

Holes won 1st half..... 2nd......Total......   Gross Score 1st half 37 2nd 35 Total 72

" lost " ......, ...Total......   Less Handicap 4

Result _____   Net Score 68

144

Length of Course 5373 Yards. Competition... Vixen Hunting Medal Scratch Score. 75 / Bogey 75

Name of Player...Miss Mary Moore... Handicap ...4... Strokes...............

Marker's Signature...J. Gould........ Date 15.9.37

Hole	Length yards	Bogey	Stroke Index	Score	Result	Hole	Length yards	Bogey	Stroke Index	Score	Result
1	380	5	7	5		10	130	3	16	3	
2	151	3	17	3		11	298	4	8	5	
3	335	4	3	3		12	410	5	2	4	
4	434	5	11	5		13	272	4	12	4	
5	385	5	5	5		14	131	3	10	3	
6	129	3	15	3		15	409	5	4	4	
7	394	5	9	5		16	110	3	18	3	
8	304	4	1	4		17	386	5	6	4	
9	319	4	13	5		18	396	5	14	5	
Tls	2,831	38		38		Tls	2,542	37		35	

BOGEY PLAY. **MEDAL PLAY.**

Holes won 1st half..... 2nd..(...Total...... Gross Score 1st half 38 2nd 35 Total 73

lost... .. ..Total... Less Handicap 4

Result Net Score 69

STRATFORD-ON-AVON GOLF CLUB (Ladies' Section)

	PLAYER(S)	Handicap	Strokes received	
A	H. ATKINSON	7		Competition Medal
(B)				Date 4.12.55
				Standard Scratch Score L.G.U. 72

Markers score	Hole	Yards	Metres	Index	Par	Gross Score A	Gross Score (B)	Net points	Markers score	Hole	Yards	Metres	Index	Par	Gross Score A	Gross Score (B)	Net points
5	1	351	321	11	4	5			3	10	148	135	14	3	3		
3	2	151	138	17	3	3			5	11	344	315	2	4	5		
	3	387	354	1	4	4				12	433	396	8	5	5		
	4	334	306	3	4	4				13	321	293	12	4	4		
	5	397	363	9	5	4				14	147	134	16	3	3		
	6	131	120	15	3	3				15	454	415	4	5	5		
	7	397	363	7	5	5				16	114	104	18	3	3		
	8	312	285	5	4	4				17	415	380	10	5	5		
5	9	306	280	13	4	5				18	435	398	6	5	4		
	Out	2766	2530		Out 36	37				In	2811	2570		In 37	37		
										Out	2766	2530		Out 36	37		
										Total	5577	5100		Total 73	74		

Marker's Signature

Player's Signature M. Atkinson

BOGEY

Holes won

Holes lost

Result

HANDICAP 7

NET SCORE 67

STABLEFORD POINTS

STRATFORD-ON-AVON GOLF CLUB (Ladies' Section)

	PLAYER(S)	Handicap	Strokes received	
A	Miss S Morgan	+1		Competition — Silver Div Medal
(B)				Date — 2.5.90
				Standard Scratch Score — L.G.U. 72

Markers score	Hole	Yards	Metres		Par	GROSS SCORE A	(B)	Net +0 pts	Markers score	Hole	Yards	Metres		Par	GROSS SCORE A	(B)	Net pts
4	1	351	321	11	4	4			4	10	148	135	14	3	3		
5	2	151	138	17	3	4			5	11	344	315	2	4	5		
5	3	387	354	1	4	4			7	12	433	396	8	5	5		
5	4	334	306	3	4	4			5	13	321	293	12	4	4		
6	5	397	363	9	5	4			4	14	147	134	16	3	3		
4	6	131	120	15	3	3			6	15	454	415	4	5	4		
5	7	397	363	7	5	4			5	16	114	104	18	3	2		
4	8	312	285	5	4	5			5	17	415	380	10	5	4		
5	9	306	280	13	4	4			6	18	435	398	6	5	4		
	Out	2766	2530	Out	36	36				In	2811	2570	In	37	34		

Marker's Signature — Bogey

S. Timberlake

Player's Signature

A Morgan

T. Minshull. Hon. Comp. Sec.

Holes won	In	2811 2570 In 37 34
Holes lost	Out	2766 2530 Out 36 36
Result	Total	5577 5100 Total 73 70 ✓
	HANDICAP	
	NET SCORE	
	STABLEFORD POINTS	71

Page 144. Ladies Course Records 1932 & 1934
Page 145. Ladies Course Records 1937 & 1985
Page 146. Ladies Course Record May 1990

The Course Today

If Samuel Ryder were able to come to Stratford today and see the course at Tiddington Road as it is, one wonders what he would think of it.

It has changed so much since the official opening in 1928 when he arranged those splendid exhibition matches by the Ryder Cup players and the leading amateur golfers of that time. In 1928 there were barely any trees on the course and from the club house it was possible to see and identify players on almost every hole. All that has now changed and although there are many more players on the course at any one time, it is now only possible to see people on the 9th and 18th.

So many trees and shrubs have been planted to define each hole and to beautify the course. It would take a qualified botanist to identify all the different species, but the enthusiastic amateur would quickly notice fir, birch, oak, sycamore, broom, beech, acacia, chestnut, acer, laburnum, silver birch and cherry.

The end of winter and the onset of spring is heralded with a riot of colour from the blossoming cherries, followed by the laburnums. The many daffodils planted amongst them add to the splash of yellow and are a sight to behold. Following the summer, as the days shorten, the gradual changing of the colours to the reds and russets of autumn is something to see. More than one member has said that the colours vie with the fall in North America, for sheer beauty.

As if all these trees were not sufficient of a hazard there are 76 bunkers to test even the best golfer.

From the tees of the day the course is 6309 yards long. There are five par "three" holes and five par "five": every one of these being under 490 yards. The long hitters are aiming to be on these greens in two shots.

Possibly because of the length of these holes many players form the opinion that it is an easy course. But even the professionals have not succeeded in making a monkey of it.

The course records are: Professional – M Gallagher 64: Amateur – Ian Roberts 65. A score of 63 was done by Andrew Jones which does not count for the record as he played off the forward tee at the 15th hole.

147

One of the reasons that the record is not lower is possibly the five par "three" holes. These will test the most skilful player. Without a doubt the best is the 16th; but the second and sixth are also a severe test. Club selection is most important, followed by a straight and true shot.

If you can finish a round having dropped only two shots at the par "threes", you will have done very well, and should have the making of a good score.

Four of the five par "fives" come in the second nine. All are well bunkered with the exception of the 12th, where there are none. From the tee, position is all important. On the 12th, a dog leg, there are two spinneys, one left and the other right. The long hitter has to gamble his shot and aim over the right spinney if he wants to have a chance of reaching the green in two.

At the 13th, par four, placement of the drive is all important. The long hitter may attempt to fly his shot over the wood on the right, to get close to the punch bowl green, and have a chance of a short pitch over the two bunkers guarding the green on the right. But this line is fraught with danger as Christy O'Connor (Senior) discovered, when playing in the Seniors Championship of 1984, when he attempted to go over the wood and ended up taking thirteen shots at this hole. Was that a record or just a coincidence?

Golfing Feats

Regrettably the Club records of golfing feats are far from complete so far as the first half century of the Club is concerned. It is only from 1950 and onwards that any real records are available and for this we have to thank Peter Rodgers who for so many years has served the Club as Competition Secretary and who continues to do so as this history is being written.

So apart from odd references to golfing successes which have appeared in the general narrative this section has to be confined to the period 1950 to 1994.

In that period the Club has produced some very good golfers.

Clive Morgan was without doubt the golfer of the two decades 1950 to 1970. He joined the Club as a junior when living on Loxley

Road, alongside the third hole. In 1950 he was in his early twenties and between 1950 and 1970 he won the Club Championship 5 times; Box Cup three times, thereby winning it outright. He represented the Cup to the Club and it is now known as the Box Morgan Cup. He also won the Docker Cup; Red Horse Cup twice; Town Bowl; Saville Cup, and in partnership with Peter Rodgers won the Gaydon Trophy in consecutive years. He left the Club in 1971 when he went to live in New Zealand.

Other golfers of note in this period were Alec Bain, Tom Stewart, twice the Club Champion, Bill Evans who was Club Champion once but who won the Coronation Scratch Cup four times.

Bob Collett, the only one to win the Town Bowl in successive years.

1970 onwards saw Tom Stewart in his prime, winning the Club Championship twice; Coronation Scratch Cup five times, Docker Cup and Shakespeare Cup.

Peter Rodgers was very prominent in this period winning the Club Championship twice; both Coronation Cups; Kendall Cup twice; Gaydon Trophy twice; Shakespeare Cup and Foursomes Matchplay twice.

The late 70s saw the Mid Warwickshire League Team win its first honour by winning the scratch prize on finals day.

The end of the 70s saw some very good juniors come through who were to dominate the 80s. Most prominent were Nick Tarrant who has won the Club Championship a record nine times, and the Coronation Scratch Cup four times. Philip James, Club Champion twice. Andrew Dunbar twice Club Champion and winner of the Coronation Scratch Cup five times. John Whitehead, once Club Champion and winner of the Coronation Scratch Cup twice. Neil Dainton winner of both Club Championship and Coronation Cup once.

In the late 80s a teenager, Andrew Jones, came on the scene and won the Club Championship and Coronation Scratch Cup in 1988. When his parents moved to Wrexham he also joined that Club and became a Welsh National Team player and then in 1991 he turned professional. Others joining the professional ranks were Andrew Dunbar, Neil Dainton and John Whitehead who returned to the amateur ranks after trying his luck on the circuit for five years.

149

1980 Stratford-on-Avon Juniors won the South Warwickshire Junior Cup for the third time.

1986 Pip Elson played for the Bells Scotch PGA club professionals team against the USA club professionals at Knollwood, Chicago.

1987 Gareth Hughes (Captain) and Pip Elson (professional) won through to the final of the Hennessy Cognac competition,played in the Bahamas, finishing 2nd. In the regional qualifying round at Coventry Golf Club, Gareth had a hole in one at the 15th hole using a number two Iron which he had bought from Pip earlier that day. This was his first shot with that club.

1989 In May, A Dunbar, N Tarrett and A Jones won the Warwickshire Team Championship at Leamington and County Golf Club. The same team played in the EGU Championship later in the year.

1989 Andrew Jones was selected as a reserve for Wales in the Amateur International in July. In the same month he, along with Andrew Rudkin and Martin Seddon won the Warwickshire Colts Team Championship.

1990 Christopher Gibbs won the Daily Telegraph Young Golfer of

Hole in one clinches a 61 and Bahamas prize

Stratford captain Gareth Hughes has amazingly scored his second hole-in-one in two days to clinch a trip to the Bahamas for the final of the Henessy Cognac Pro-Am.

Hughes's ace at the 201yd 15th hole at Coventry Finham yesterday helped Stratford professional Tip Elson compile a 12-under-par net 61 for a two-shot victory over the host club.

The previous day, while Elson was winning the Warwickshire professional title at Kenilworth, Hughes had been celebrating the third hole-in-one of his career at Langland Bay in Wales where he was on holiday with his wife.

Before leaving Stratford yesterday morning, Elson informed the 58-year-old club captain that a new two-iron club he had or-

dered ten weeks ago had been delivered.

"He asked me if I wanted to take it with me to Coventry, and if so which club did I want to leave out. But as I only had 13 in my bag instead of the maximum 14, I said I would take it there and then," said Hughes.

"But it wasn't until we got to the 15th hole, which is either a two- or three-iron shot, that I considered using it for the first time. I had one practice swing before hitting the ball off the tee and was astounded to see it hit the green and disappear into the hole.

"To hole in one the first time you use a club is incredible in itself. But to do it the day after another is just unbelievable."

Birmingham Post report July 1987

150

Chris Gibbs
Photo: Ann Gibbs

151

Monday, May 17, 1993

Nick keeps so cool in the heat of Dubai

Master stroke: Stratford's current club champion Nick Tarratt who is golf manager at the Emirates Club in Dubai.

Golf around the region – Coventry Evening Telegraph report 17th May 1993

WHEN Nick Tarratt makes his annual excursion to Stratford it is a case of "Hello and Dubai!"

Because the 33-year old has made a habit of breezing in from his job as golf manager at the Emirates Club in Dubai, and walking off with the club championship.

"I've won it for the last four years," admitted the former Warwickshire County player. "And eight times n all. People think that because I work out here I play golf all the time. Rest assured nothing could be further from the truth."

Tarratt, in fact, manages on average to play 18 holes once a month on that extraordinary green oasis in the middle of the desert.

The rest of his time is largely consumed by the demands of running a top quality, now world renowned complex.

"65,000 rounds of golf are played here each year," said Tarratt, who took up the post in Dubai on the advice of former boss Colin Snape.

"And given it gets dark at 5.30pm in the winter then you can imagine that is a lot of golf in out peak period.

"We also have international groups here and a number of tournaments including of course the Dubai Desert Classic which is the highlight of the Club's calendar.

"But there has been a really big change recently with the development of two new courses, the Creek Golf Club and the Dubai Racing Club – which will open later in the year.

"It means that we have switched from being a busy members" club to being more of a golf resort.

"We're very keen to promote golf in Dubai as a destination and resort where you can now play seven days a week.

"Before it was difficult because we did not have the tee times or space available to accommodate a large number of visitors."

A green fee at the multi-million pound complex with one of the most photographed clubhouses in the

---

"People think that because I work out here I play golf all the time. Rest assured nothing could be further from the truth."

Nick Tarratt

---

world, would set you back – according to the exchange rate – between £40 and £50.

Tee off times start at 6.20am for those wishing to avoid the heat of the day and run through to early evening.

"Temperatures get up to about 120F in the height of the summer," said Tarratt, who admits that he has become acclimatised in the three years since he took up the job.

"But because of the water and the trees on the course it never gets unbearable."

The fairways, greens and tees of the Emirates club are kept in pristine and flourishing order thanks to more than a million gallons of water that are pumped on to the course – per day!

Fifty-five greenkeeping staff are also employed to ensure the highest of standards are maintained.

Because of the success of the facility, golf is becoming increasingly popular throughout the Gulf.

But because it is a relatively new sport, standards that are commonplace in Britain, have had to be introduced.

"That was one of the hardest parts of my job when I first came out here," added Tarratt, who worked at the PGA for five years.

"The etiquette, rules and regulations that are handed down by senior members at a club in England, didn't exist in the same way because there weren't any senior players.

"So I had to set about improving things like slow play, dress regulations, where you can drive the carts – that sort of thing. It was the only way forward."

Tarratt intends to stay in Dubai, which will again stage the Desert Classic next year, for the foreseeable future.

"I do get a little homesick from time to time," he admitted. "The ex-pats way of life is an acquired one but I'm getting used to it and now we"ve got satellite television things have improved enormously.

"The golf tournaments are usually a week or so behind but at least we get some sport now.

"And career wise there probably aren't so many better places to be."

the year competition at Stratford, with a 68 (including three 2's), which qualified him for the final played at Pennina, Portugal, in which he finished eighth. Aged 15 he was the second youngest of the 15 qualifiers. During the summer he brought his handicap down from five to three in six weeks and won the John Preston Memorial Cup in the Midland Boys Championship and played for Warwickshire boys.

This section would not be complete without special mention of Nicky Tarrett, one of that very successful team of golfers of 1989. Not only has he won the Club Championship nine times but he has also played for Warwickshire on fifty one occasions. This is a quite remarkable achievement, particularly bearing in mind his five years absence from the Club, travelling as a PGA Tournament Controller, and two years away as Golf Secretary at the Emirates Golf Club in Dubai. He has now moved on and is General Manager, Dubai Golf and Racing Club.

Course Records

The Amateur Course Record Holders in recent years have been:
Up to 1977 – Pip Elson with a 68
From 1977 to 1990 – Peter Rodgers with a 67 – this was equalled by Neil Dainton, Nick Tarrett and Andrew Dunbar.
From 1990 – Ian Roberts with a 65
   For some years the Professional Course Record was held by John Whitehead with a 65 until it was broken in 1990 by Michael Gallagher with a 64.

County Representation

In addition to Nicky Tarrett's fifty one appearances (mentioned above) the following have all played for Warwickhire County 1st Team: Andrew Dunbar, Andrew Jones, Ian Roberts.
   The team of Nicky Tarrett, Andrew Dunbar and Andrew Jones twice won the County Team Shield and represented Warwickshire at the County National Finals.

'I Remember . . .'

Memories and Reflections of Members.

Incidents in the Club House and on the Course.

(Very sadly Pat Brownsdon did not survive to see his contributions to this section published.)

Trouble Getting Going – Pat Brownsdon

A true veteran, Lou Cook, one time Midlands Senior Champion, emerged from the locker room, via the club bar after being suitably warmed up by rather more than his usual ration of wee drams. Not that it was a dreary winter's day – far from it. The early afternoon sun was beating down remorselessly as he trundled his trolley to the tee. He felt a slight unusual weakness in his knees which he put down to the sudden exposure to bright sunlight, and the almost torrid heat of a lovely afternoon.

His three partners insisted that he play first so he confidently selected his five iron from his bag. Bending down on the tee did not feel quite right either. That day the tee happened to be right forward on the brink of the bank. After his usual waggle, he played his shot, missed the ball completely, over balanced, and rolled like a hedgehog to the bottom of the slope, finishing in the buttercups, which at,that time were in full flower. None the worse, he picked himself up, climbed the steep incline, teed up again; dead to the pin this time and down for three winning the hole.

John Waddington, who normally packs a hefty drive, teed up and with a rush of air took a terrific swipe at the ball. He caught it on the heel, hit the back of a tree on the left with a resounding clonk. The ball rebounded high in the air to the tee, where it was

155

caught full toss by the Club professional, Leslie Ball. Question: How many off the tee?

A venerable senior, Sam Pritchard, went through his usual pre match routine, getting a reasonably clean ball out of the bag, selecting his club, and took a few swings to ease the tension. The big moment arrived with a swish of the ball which was hit on the toe of the club. At that moment, his partner, Sid Newey, noticed a peculiar protusion from Sam's right heel, which elicited the advice that perhaps his second shot may be a slight improvement if he removed his shoehorn.

Captain's Bonanza 1990 – Pat Brownsdon

The last event of the 1990 season went off literally with a bang. A lady looking bleary eyed out of her kitchen window saw a bright flash in the semi darkness of the December morning, followed by a puff of black smoke – the shot gun start of the Captain's Bonanza was under way.

The non golfing lady, however, alerted the police who immediately got in touch with the Golf Club, only to find it deserted with practically the whole membership out on the course trying to keep their heads down. Not to be beaten the police considered the incident serious enough to scramble the helicopter (at a cost of £000s) to seek out the mystery intruders who were bombarding the town at such an unearthly hour on a Sunday morning.

All manner of dread happenings were dreamed up – the IRA were embattled on the Welcombe Hills; something was being dropped from outer space, or nearer the mark, someone was letting off surplus fireworks. Headlines appeared in the "Herald" with the alarmist suggestion "Mystery Bang over Stratford". All this, notwithstanding that a good posse of the Stratford Police Force were, at the very time the helicopter appeared overhead, doing their best to get out of the sand, or get their putts down in their keenness to take home the hotly contested Bonanza.

No doubt it is good to know that our guardians of the law and order are really on the ball when faced with an incident of such genuine gravity.

One Fine Day – Pat Brownsdon

There were many beautiful warm and sunny days in 1974. On one of these, one of our senior members, who had better remain incognito, had invited three visitors for a game. The sunny day and refreshment in the club house created a feeling of high euphoria and as they loosened up on the tenth tee no thought was given to the unfortunate, though not entirely unpredictable, outcome.

Having delved in their bags for an uncut ball and agreed the stakes, they were pointed in the right direction by the irascible senior as well as given advice on clubbing. One ball soared into the trees on the right. Another kicked off the bank into the left hand bunker, and the other two failed to make the bank. No great improvement on the 11th. In fact this "halcyon" round was heading for trouble, big trouble. It was slowing down – ball searching on the 12th, not the best thing for one's health and temper, particularly when the "Famous Grouse" is wearing off.

Worse was to come. Out of the corner of his eye the irascible senior could see what he imagined to be two young men approaching fast down the 12th fairway. The four stood their ground, drove off the 13th tee. Two on the fairway, the other two in the spinney on the right.

The "young men" were on the tee.

Hacking out of the trees, shots to the green, a lengthy putting session, and not a glimmer of a backward glance, or the hint of a call through. On to the 14th tee and down to the green with patience behind them boiling over. One of the pair left his trolley and came across to confront the four duffers and asked them whether they had ever heard of the etiquette of golf or even the courtesy of the course. The irascible one enquired who on earth he thought he was. He was not going to be spoken to like that by a mere whippersnapper, particularly in the presence of important guests. The young man identified himself as Captain of the Club, who indeed he was. This deflationary reply won a hasty, ill tempered let through, followed by hurriedly written apologetic letters to various Committee friends in a bid to escape the dreaded sanction of ignominious expulsion from the Club.

A warning and a second chance was all that could be salvaged from this fateful round of golf in high summer.

Moral – try to remember the cut of the Captain's jib.

Happy Recollections of a Long Association with Stratford-on-Avon Golf Club – Jack Mound

I became a member of Stratford-on-Avon Golf Club in 1955, but long before that, I had associations with the Club going back to the very early days at Tiddington Road.

As a twelve year old schoolboy I helped on the course, first by picking stones off the fairways, for which I was paid 3d per hour. Occasionally on the fifth fairway I would find a Roman coin. These were handed to the Secretary Mr Shimell Andrew who gave me 6d per coin. Later I became a caddie and attended the Club on Saturday and Sunday along with 20/30 other boys, all hoping to be employed.

I remember on one match day, a visitor from Cheltenham, Mr Humphreys, asking me to fetch balls on the practice ground. He then asked me to caddie for him in the match and gave me 2/6 for my lunch. After 18 holes we came in for tea and I was given 1/-. After tea another nine holes were played and I was paid 7/-. I had received a total of 10/6 and I felt like a millionaire.

On leaving school my first job was assistant to John Humphreys, the steward and I was paid 10/- per week. Later I was sacked as the Club could not afford to employ me, and so I went to work for Mr Andrew, the Secretary, doing odd jobs about his house at Shottery. I also went up to the Club to help my schoolfriend, Nobby Clarke, who was employed in the professional's shop, working for Len Leach.

I well remember the "Golfing Week" when all competitions were played in one week, two per day, finishing with the Town Bowl on the Saturday.

The greenkeeper, Tom Ryman, who lived in the cottage near the barn, and had seven children, made a little business by picking the mushrooms off the course and selling them to a local greengrocer.

Ships that Pass in the Night – A S (Freddie) Walker

Two outstanding golfers who, sadly, were members for too short a time, came into the Club in 1969 and I think 1976. One died and the other was moved on by his employer long before their names would normally have reached the top of the waiting list.

It was on a cold and wet Saturday morning that I drove into the car park with the intention of picking up a game. There were few cars and no members in sight. A stranger appeared and asked me the way to the pro's shop. I took him round to Leslie Ball, learning as we walked that he had just been moved to the area from South Wales. He had decided that Stratford was the club he would most like to join. Mr Ball suggested that the visitor might like to play the course with me while he, Leslie, would obtain an application form from the Secretary. He felt obliged to point out, however, that the waiting list was of the order of 4–5 years.

As we were walking out of his shop Leslie asked him his handicap and the reply was "Two".

By the time we had played 18 holes and changed our clothes, we were met by two or three Committee members and David Burgess was "interviewed" a few days later. He was elected to membership at the next meeting of the main Committee and won the Club Championship that year. He was also at that time, joint record holder at the St Pierre Golf Club. Not long after, the Steel Company of Wales moved him on.

It was in 1976 I think, that I spotted a Walker Cup blazer badge on a stranger standing at the bar and on introducing myself discovered that he had recently put in an application to join the Stratford-on-Avon Golf Club. As a result of this chance meeting Jimmy Wilson was invited to talk to the Membership Committee a few days later. He was encouraged to talk about his golf and it was a remarkable story. He had been a schoolboy champion and twice, a Scottish finalist. He had played everywhere it seemed and was at one time coached by Tommy Armour. At a St Andrews centenary he broke the course record and was awarded a gold medal. His record was not improved upon for 23 years! He was given a handicap of plus two (or was it more?). When asked his handicap he replied "Och I haven't really got one now it is so long since I played golf, but I could play off two or three if you like – that should be fairly comfortable!" He was a revelation to play with (especially in a strong wind) and within a very short time he won a Club competition. Against par he was quite a few "up".

He was only able to play for a short while and sadly died (in his mid 60s, I think).

My Early Days at Tiddington Road – Leslie Ball

When I started with the Club as its professional in 1962, succeeding Len Leach, there were so few trees on the course, that all players could be seen from the club house. Very different from today.

So few people played in those days that I was able to give lessons on the first fairway. There was no need to go to the practice ground. Often there would be only six or so people on the course.

I started at 9 am and went home at 6 pm in midsummer. On Sundays I would lock up at 3 pm as so few players were about. Nobody started before 9 am in the 1960's and I remember an entry in the suggestion book that the professional should start at 8-30 am.

All this changed rapidly when Pat Barrett started his "Dawn Patrol", along with Laurie Dobson, Tom Pargetter and Archie Pooler, at 8 am or earlier.

In the winter I gave them coffee in the professional's shop waiting for daylight. Then when the weather was bad Pat Barrett would go up to the first hole, take a look at it and decide to close the course.

Two for the Guinness Book of Records? – John Gee

Mid-air Collision

A quite extraordinary incident took place one Sunday morning in the 1970s.

I was playing in a four-ball and had started at the 10th hole. Standing on the 11th tee I watched my partner Reg Watson prepare to play his tee shot. He drove off and skied his ball, high in the air.

Instinctively my eyes followed the ball as it soared away from the tee. It began to drop and then to my astonishment I saw it collide with another ball at about sixty feet. This second ball had come from the 10th tee at right angles. John Whitehead playing in the match behind us had hit his ball clean over the 10th green and it was heading for the rugby field when this amazing collision took place. The odds against this happening must be incalculable, even by John and his computers.

I wonder if this has ever happened before or whether it would qualify for the Guinness Book of Records?

What a Birdie!

One Wednesday morning in the 1980s I was playing a friendly four-ball with Eric Andrew, Cliff Glascoe, and Joe Mawle. On the 15th hole my tee shot finished in the first bunker, on the right. My second shot went straight into the next row of bunkers, and my third into the further bunker on the left of the green. From there my fourth shot went straight into the hole. In three bunkers on one hole! What a way to get a Birdie! How many times has this happened?

Violet Simpson (Life Member and Vice President) in her 68th Year of Membership Recalls:–

Trixie Gould

"Trixie Gould's progress on the fairway in competitions was frequently marked by an upright feather, which became her personal identification mark. It was not unusual either, to hear a sharp explosion when Trixie struck her ball on the tee. A matchstick strategically hidden behind her tee-peg, or diddy, took the full force of the blow."

161

The Westwood Cup

"One afternoon in 1947 a rare flutter on the horses brought a win for Mrs Westwood. Mr Edmund Chaumeton, who was present among the party, suggested that she might like to celebrate by donating a cup to the Ladies' Section. That was the origin of the Westwood Cup."

Mrs Simpson (Violet's mother) and Bridge

'It seems that 'Ma' Simpson was as enthusiastic about bridge as she was about golf. Her partnership with Dr Arnold during the Second World War was a very formidable one; in fact their RAF opponents at the Golf Club becoming tired of defeat at the table sought revenge on the golf course in a challenge match. The result can be guessed!"

Profiles

A few prominent members of the Club spanning the century.

Regrettably it has not been possible to obtain profiles of some of the more important members in the very early days.

The sad death of Peter Boddington in 1992, who was writing profiles of Brewster Norbury and Guy Pemberton dealt a severe blow to this part of the history. (Author).

Pat Barrett by Laurie Dobson

Patrick John Barrett, known to all as PB was born in Castlebar, County Mayo and came to the Stratford area in the 1940s.

A gregarious man, possessing considerable drive and energy, his ready Irish wit and humour made him a popular figure in many walks of life. Someone who always wished to be involved and with the capacity to generate enthusiasm where none had previously existed.

Pat had links with many sporting activities and was a keen racegoer and golfing enthusiast. He joined the Stratford Club when he moved to Clifford Chambers in 1951 having previously been a member of Broadway Golf Club. It was not long before he was elected to the Committee and was appointed Captain in 1958 and 1959. He later became the first "permanent" Chairman from 1964 to 1976, this office having previously been held by the incumbent Captain. In 1976 he was appointed President until his untimely death in 1982 at the age of 65. Pat had served the Club well for over 30 years.

Without question Pat contributed more to the Club than any other single person and it was entirely due to his drive and enthusiasm that the Club progressed to its present day level. He was largely responsible for organising almost all the major building projects which took place in the 1960s and 70s but also for supervising the work on a daily basis. He also acted as personal guarantor for bank loans to enable work to proceed and used his own plant and machinery to construct all the tees we have today. He undertook the supervision and maintenance of all the golf course machinery and he also sponsored the Annual Pro/AM events for several years. He became a Vice-President of the Midland PGA and was also President of the Warwickshire PGA.

It is impossible to quantify his contribution to the Club but suffice it to say that through his legendary generosity members paid considerably less in annual dues than at many other comparable local clubs.

In recognition of his services to the Club he was presented with his portrait in oils in 1976 and following his death the members raised a sum to provide the Pat Barrett Memorial Cup which is played for annually in his memory.

We shall not see his like again.

Peter Boddington by Neville Tarrett.

As many of our older members know, Peter Boddington was the epitome of the old style gentleman golfer.

I knew him in a business capacity and one day he invited me to have a round of "GOFF" (never Golf). He was in his early seventies, and when he told me his handicap it was considerably lower than I expected. I must have shown this and typically he drew himself up to his considerable height and modestly and quietly remarked, "I was Captain of Warwickshire you know".

I am sure that I learnt more about the etiquette of golf in that most enjoyable round, than in any other.

One of Peter's many concerns was why I pronounced "putt" to rhyme with "soot". My explanation that I came from Wolverhampton never really put his mind at rest!

How Peter ever found time for golf in his long and happy retirement is a mystery. A Justice of the Peace, he had been Chairman of Stratford Hospital Management Committee, whilst his passion for conservation resulted in him being appointed a Local Trustee of the Shakespeare Birthday Trust where his forthright, far-seeing views soon ensured him becoming Vice Chairman of the Executive Committee and latterly a Life Trustee, a position he held until his death in 1992, aged 84.

P B Rodgers by Richard W Olliss

Peter (Byron) Rodgers is best known to Club members in his role as Competitions Secretary, or, more correctly, Chairman of the Handicap and Competitions Committee – understandable since he has occupied that office on a continuous basis for the last 25 years.

Born in Derby on 13th June 1936, Peter attended Oakham School from the age of 12, leaving there to join the Navy where he served, without particular distinction, during the years 1954–56.

A move "out of the frying pan into the fat" took him to what proved to be his first, and only, non-military employer Van Den Berghs & Jurgens where he worked just as loyally for 31 years until his retirement in 1991.

It seems that unbroken service is the hallmark of Peter's life for having been invited to join the Golf Club Committee, as Competitions Secretary in 1968, only five years after first becoming a member, he has resolutely remained there (re-election ballots notwithstanding) in precisely the same role, including his year of captaincy in 1971, ever since. In 1993 Peter and the Club celebrated his twenty-five years in a job well done.

Club members can only admire and be grateful to Peter for the loyal service which he has given over such a long period. In fact 1993 was quite a year all round for Peter because it saw both his children Jonathan and Emma starting their own married lives.

In his time Peter has been quite a force to be reckoned with on the golf course. He held the amateur course record (67 gross) between 1977 and 1990, although he is at pains to point out that it was equalled several times during the period. His name is to be found, somewhere, on nearly all the prize winners boards around the club house, and in places more than once. The trophy which has so far eluded him, and which he still covets greatly, and not, as one might otherwise assume, with declining confidence, is the Town Bowl.

Peter's handicap, though now six was two for many years from the mid-sixties through to 1973. From then it crept up and up to a discouraging nine until his retirement in 1991. Clearly his "fat free" daily life since then has been good, not only for his health, but also his golf!

Over the years, of course, Peter has also perfected the art of the "sticky finger draw" and some of those prize presentations at the Tigers v Rabbits dinner really were a sight to behold.

Legend has it that back in 1968 a certain L G Dobson said to Peter "I've seen you hanging around the Club a lot – how would you like to be Competitions Secretary?" Well, Peter, lets hope you continue to "hang around the Club a lot" for many years to come.

Jan 94. Peter has announced that he is going to live in Spain. We shall miss him. [Author]

Lt Cdr A S.Walker (Freddie) by David Moffat

A profile of Alfred Sydney Walker, better known universally as "Freddie", is a portrait of a sportsman and a gentleman.

A sportsman, certainly – an athlete, a skilled exponent in the arts of boxing, skiing, fencing, rugby, football and, latterly golf – he nevertheless, and by the way of a bonus, had the great good fortune to be born one of nature's gentlemen, a quality which demands no further description.

Freddie was born in Portsmouth on 29th December 1912 and, to quote him, he was "a horror when young". His particular sporting inclinations in his early days were towards running, water polo and rugby football, activities which he felt could be nurtured by a career in the Royal Navy. He was a middle distance runner and champion of the Mediterranean Fleet in 1946 although it was at boxing that he achieved perhaps his greatest sporting achievements. Boxing as a lightweight he won the Inter Services Boxing Association Championship in the years 1938 and 1939. He boxed regularly for the Royal Navy and on one occasion he fought the Danish lightweight champion at the Albert Hall. He was, moreover, an excellent skier and a member of the Alpine Club and, to underline his virtuosity, he represented the Royal Navy at bayonet fencing in the Royal Tournament at Olympia.

Freddie served in the Royal Navy from 1929 to 1955, rising to the rank of Lieutenant Commander. He joined the service as a rating and, training as a telegraphist, he progressed through the ranks and was one of the very few selected for a commission. During the Second World War he served in the North Sea (1940), the North Atlantic (1941), the Mediterranean (1942 and 1943) and the Far East (1944 to 1946). In 1942, he joined a depot submarine ship in the Mediterranean and became the flotilla torpedo specialist. In the Far East he served in a light cruiser, the first ship to go back to Hong Kong, and after the war in various ships went to South Africa, Fiji, Samoa, Tonga and the Congo, until his retirement in 1955.

In that year he began work in Birmingham for a firm started by Sir Oliver Lodge and after a year or so demonstrating his entrepreneurial flair, he bought a screw stockist. He ran this business until 1982 when he sold it to begin a long and fruitful retirement.

In 1939 Freddie married Lillian, herself later to become an enthusiastic golfer who became Ladies Captain in 1978; they have two children, Simon and Mark. In 1960 the family moved to Tiddington and in 1965 Freddie designed and built the house there, in which they still live.

Freddie joined Stratford-on-Avon Golf Club in the early 1960s having, by his own admission, become hugely enthusiastic about the game. He rapidly acquired membership of four clubs in addition to our own – Broadway, St Pierre, Moseley and an overseas membership of La Moye, Jersey – a quite unbelievable achievement by today's standards. At Stratford-on-Avon he has held with great distinction the offices of President (1989–1992) and Captain (1981) and he served the Club for many years as a member of the Board of Directors and, his particular interest, as Chairman of the Green Committee. He is a most competitive golfer, instincts which have served him well in numerous competitions over the years.

Further he was a founder member and a Council member of the Society of Warwickshire Golf Captains, a highly successful society

167

of captains and past-captains boasting a membership of some 300, which Freddie himself captained in 1989.

Always immaculately attired and bubbling with enthusiasm, Freddie is a man of immense charm and wit. His fund of stories is legendary and those of us privileged to have heard "Able Seaman 'awkins" (on perhaps more than one occasion!) or the tale of the elephants are unlikely ever to forget them. A most accomplished man, a great character and a man to whom Stratford-on-Avon Golf Club owes a considerable debt.

Dennis Whitehouse – President 1992–93 by Vic Burn.

Dennis Whitehouse enjoyed the honour and privilege of his Presidency, and indeed in preparation for Centenary Year wrote a message, which due to his untimely death in March 1993 cannot now be published. It is however appropriate, and a tribute to him that quotations from his script should be included in this appreciation.

Reference is made to his first visit to Stratford-upon-Avon some sixty years ago, when as a boy scout from Coventry, his troop camped on what was a disused green of the old golf course on the Welcombe Hills.

In a more contemporary vein, a request is made for the full support from all members during Centenary Year, and a conclusion in which the words of an earlier President are quoted, "Don't ask what can the Club do for me, but what can I do for the Club?"

Dennis was a wholehearted person, unequivocal, always concerned with maintaining high standards of behaviour and dress both on the course and in the club house.

The playing of sports had complemented his life from school through to retirement. Always a competitor he preferred in his earlier years team games, and at King Henry VIII Grammar School he played First XV Rugby and Coventry First X1 Cricket, and later scrum half for the Old Coventrians and wicket-keeper batsman for Coventry and North Warwickshire.

After cricket he turned to golf following the example of his parents who were both members of Hearsall Golf Club. He became a keen exponent of the game and played to a high standard, being a member of several clubs; Hearsall, Long Ashton and Norwich, and finally Stratford-on-Avon some 23 years ago when he was appointed General Sales Manager of Dunlop Tyre Company in Birmingham and took up residence in Stratford-upon-Avon. In recent years he became a country member of Weston-Super-Mare.

He retired some 14 years ago, played more golf and gave his time in running the affairs of the Club, being a member of the Committee, Chairman of Green and for five years Chairman of the Committee. He enjoyed every facet of the Club; the playing, the social attributes and administration, but most of all he treasured his office of President, and it is sad that he did not live for the celebration of our Centenary Year, but he will be remembered by so many who had the privilege of knowing him and who are grateful for his efforts on behalf of the Club.

Stanley Tyas by Ted Marson

Stanley Tyas was a member of Stratford-on-Avon Golf Club for over forty years. He was born in Clayton West, Huddersfield, and after completing his education became an accountant with the local Co-operative Society.

During the early part of the Second World War, he joined the Royal Air Force and served with distinction as a Squadron Leader, adjutant, with No 152 (Hyderabad) Squadron flying Spitfires in Burma and India.

Shortly after the War he moved to the Stratford area as Manager of the Bidford and Mickleton Co-operative Society. Later he became a partner in Coleman and Tyas, builders and eventually merged this company with another to create the Espley Tyas construction group, with Stan as its Deputy Chairman.

As a tribute to his ability he was subsequently appointed President of the Federation of Master Builders.

Stan had an active interest in many sports such as cricket, tennis, horse racing, but with golf his first love. He was also a very keen bridge player attending bridge conventions all over the world.

One of the highlights of his golfing years was to play against his two sons in the final of the Gaydon Trophy, winter league. Unfortunately

Stan was on the losing side after a fiercely fought contest. He was a founder member of the Avon Golf Society which recently celebrated its 40th anniversary.

He was always an enthusiastic member of the Stratford-on-Avon Golf Club serving for many years as a Director in many capacities and at the same time ensuring that the Golf Club traditions were maintained. He was honoured and proud to be elected Club Captain in 1962.

With two sons and a daughter Stan was a devoted family man. One of his sons, Phillip, is still a well known member of the Club.

The Club owes considerable thanks to Stanley Tyas for his devoted service over many years. His untimely death in 1992 has left a distinct gap in the Club for the Centenary Year.

Epilogue

Message from the Chairman
– Mr S H Thomas

I welcome this opportunity to record the members' appreciation to all those who have helped in making this book so interesting. It portrays a factual record of events which have helped in shaping Stratford-on-Avon Golf Club.

Quite rightly the book identifies many who have made significant contributions, but I feel a great debt is owed by us all to those ordinary members who have supported the Club through the years.

We are now on the threshold of the next century and I am sure the years to come will be equally as great as those which have passed.

A particular tribute to John Gee who has diligently devoted the past three years to the research and collation of the details of our history, and presented them in this most interesting book.

Stratford-on-Avon Golf Club Captains

Year	Name
1896–1901	G F Kendall
1902–1903	T H Lloyd
1904–1905	D B Sanders
1906–1908	B Norbury
1909	W F Hutchings
1910	D W Evans
1911–1914	G Pemberton
1915–1918	The Great War Period – No Captain Elected
1919–1920	G Pemberton
1921–1923	S B S Walker

1924	P H Wells
1925–1927	B Norbury
1928	R W T Kendall
1929–1930	S Ryder
1931	G H Champ
1932	W F Box
1933	Sir A D Flower
1934	Fred Sedgewick
1935	H M Crawford
1936–1937	Spenser Flower
1938	E A Barnard
1939	C W Pardoe
1940–1945	World War II – No Captain Elected
1946	A E Titchmarsh
1947	E E Chaumeton
1948	J Blower
1949	H Hardman
1950	Sir Edward Salt
1951	J E S Lockwood
1952	A F Brownlow
1953	Sidney Booth
1954	F W M Workman
1955	A F Jordan
1956	N Ashworth
1957	W Harvey
1958	P Barrett
1959	P Barrett
1960	R Robinson
1961	C W Wilkins
1962	S Tyas
1963	S/Ldr A D Bain
1964	Tom Pargetter
1965	G C Luker
1966	F J Kitchen
1967	L G Dobson
1968	E Kerby
1969	Capt J Stretton-Cox
1970	Wilfred Rookes

1971	P B Rodgers
1972	G R T Collett
1973	H F Field
1974	M J E Harrison
1975	G L R Cartwright
1976	A Hanks
1977	D A Davies
1978	A Saunders
1979	S C Scriven
1980	W E Marson
1981	Lt Cdr A S Walker
1982	Richard W Ollis
1983	D C Moffat
1984	M A F Gregg
1985	V L Burn
1986	John W Gee
1987	G R Hughes
1988	P R Clarke
1989	P J Miles
1990	H W Rushmere
1991	S H Thomas
1992	P Clayton
1993	F G Prentice
1994	C Walford

Presidents

1897–1911	Sir George O Trevelyan Bart
1912–1924	Rev Francis H Hodgson
1925–1935	Ludford C Docker Esq JP
1936–1950	Sir Archie D Flower
1951–1952	Sir Martin Melvin Bart
1953–1963	Major R Y T Kendall
1964–1970	E C Glover Esq
1971–1975	E E Chaumeton Esq
1976–1982	P Barrett Esq
1983–1985	L G Dobson Esq

1986–1988	E Kerby Esq
1989–1991	A S Walker Esq
1992–1993	D Whitehouse Esq
1993–	L G Dobson Esq

Principal Trophies

Pat Barrett Memorial Trophy
Box Morgan Cup
Club Championship Cup
Coronation Cup
Coronation Goblet
Docker Cup
Foursomes Matchplay Cup
Gaydon Trophy
Kendall Cup
Mixed Foursomes Matchplay Trophy
Saville Cup
Scratch Matchplay Trophy
Seniors Cup
Sheldon Bowl
Silverman Cup
Town Bowl
Veterans Cup
Victory Trophy
Past Captains Trophy

Club Champions

1952	W Harvey
1953	R Robinson
1954	W Harvey
1955	D L Gould
1956	R Robinson
1957	E St J Salt

1958	C C Morgan
1959	N Gracey
1960	C C Morgan
1961	D J W Lampard
1962	C C Morgan
1963	P J Busby
1964	A D Bain
1965	A D Bain
1966	P J Busby
1967	C C Morgan
1968	C C Morgan
1969	D E Burgess
1970	E W Evans
1971	T Stewart
1972	T Stewart
1973	E W Evans
1974	S T Johnson
1975	P B Rodgers
1976	D N Tarratt
1977	P B Rodgers
1978	T N J Parry
1979	D N Tarratt
1980	D N Tarratt
1981	D N Tarratt
1982	N C F Dainton
1983	A J Dunbar
1984	P D James
1985	P D James
1986	J Whitehead
1987	A J Dunbar
1988	A Jones
1989	D N Tarratt
1990	D N Tarratt
1991	D N Tarratt
1992	D N Tarratt
1993	D N Tarratt

						H CAP	Strokes Rec'd						

PLAYER A *MICHAEL GALLAGHER*

PLAYER B

COMPETITION *PRO - AM*

DATE *16 TH SEPT 1990*

SSS (White) 70 (Yellow) 69

Par 72

Marker's Score	Hole	Length yards	Par	Stroke Index	S				Hole	Length yards	Par	Stroke Index	SSS A	Score B	
	1	361	4	9	3				10	154	3	16	3		
	2	168	3	17	3				11	367	4	6	4		
	3	400	4	7	4				12	479	5	2	6		
	4	421	4	1	4				13	355	4	12	4		
	5	402	4	5	4				14	205	3	14	3		
	6	181	3	15	3				15	476	5	4	3		
	7	490	5	3	4				16	151	3	18	2		
	8	363	4	11	4				17	476	5	10	4		
	9	381	4	13	3				18	479	5	8	3		
	Total	3167	35	Out	32				Total	3142	37	In	32		

Marker's Signature *BurDonald.*

Player's Signature *M. Gally*

	3167	35	Out 32
	6309	72	Total 64

Holes won		Handicap		
Holes lost		Net score		
PAR RESULT		Stableford points		

Course Record – Professional

176

					H.CAP	Strokes Rec'd										
PLAYER A	/ ROBERTS					2		COMPETITION		TERRY RAVEL PM.						
PLAYER B								DATE	23rd SEPTEMBER 1940							
SSS (White) 70 (Yellow) 69						Best Ball Net Win + Loss - Half 0 Points		Par 72							Best Ball Net Win + Loss - Half 0 Points	
Marker's Score	Hole	Length Yards	Par	Stroke Index	Gross A	Score B		Marker's Score	Hole	Length Yards	Par	Stroke Index	Gross A	Score B		
	1	361	4	9	4				10	154	3	16	3			
	2	168	3	17	5				11	367	4	6	3			
	3	400	4	7	4				12	479	5	2	3			
	4	421	4	1	3				13	355	4	12	6			
	5	402	4	5	4				14	205	3	14	3			
	6	181	3	15	3				15	476	5	4	4			
	7	490	5	3	4				16	151	3	18	2			
	8	363	4	11	5				17	476	5	10	4			
	9	381	4	13	4				18	479	5	8	4			
	Total	3167	35	Out	34				Total	3142	37	In	31			
Marker's Signature										3167	35	Out	34			
										6309	72	Total	65			
Player's Signature						Holes won			Handicap	2						
						Holes lost			Net score	63						
						PAR RESULT			Stableford points							

Course Record – Amateur

177

PLAYER A	A V. JONES		HCAP	T 1	Strokes Rec'd		COMPETITION	MEDAL N° 7

PLAYER B

DATE 11 08 90

| SSS (White) 70 (Yellow) 69 | | | | | | | Par 72 | | | | | |

Marker's Score	Hole	Length Yards	Par	Stroke Index	Length A	Score B	best for Net Points Loss Match Points	Marker's Score	Hole	Length Yards	Par	Stroke Index	Length	Score	best for Net Points Loss Match Points
	1	361	4	9	3				10	154	3	16	4		
	2	168	3	17	3				11	367	4	6	3		
	3	400	4	7	4				12	479	5	2	4		
	4	421	4	1	4				13	355	4	12	4		
	5	402	4	5	3				14	205	3	14	2		
	6	181	3	15	3				15	415.1	4	4	4		
	7	490	5	3	4				16	151	3	18	4		
	8	363	4	11	3				17	476	5	10	3		
	9	381	4	13	3				18	479	5	8	5		
Total		3167	35	Out	30			Total		3122	35	In	33		

Marker's Signature	M. B. Grinstead			3167	35	Out	30
				62..	7?	Total	63

Player's Signature	A V Jones	Holes won		Handicap	+ 1
		Holes lost		Net score	64
		PAR RESULT		Stableford points	

Andrew Jones' score – 11th August 1990

178

Bibliography

Sources

Stratford-on-Avon Golf Club — Minutes 30/6/1894 – Date
Stratford-on Avon Golf Club
Ladies' Section — Minutes 8/4/1899 to date.
The Shakespeare Birthplace Trust — Stratford-upon-Avon
   Records Office — Archives

Books and Publications

Donald Steel — The Guinness Book of Golf Feats and Facts
Corporation of Stratford-upon-Avon and the Trustees of Shakespeare's
   Birthplace — A Romano British Industrial Settlement near Tiddington,
   Stratford-upon-Avon
Robert Bearman — The Welcombe Hotel. — Focus Vol 2 No 9   March 1980
Stratford-upon-Avon Official Guide 1908
Golf Today 1992
Ryder Cup Programme 1985
Ladies Golf Union Official Year Book 1929

Journals

Birmingham Gazette 1896–1958
Birmingham Post 1929–1989
Coventry Evening Telegraph 1993
Coventry Standard 1894
Evesham Journal and Four Shires Advertiser 1930
Stratford-upon-Avon Herald 1894–1978

Oral Reminiscences

Leslie Ball
The late Peter Boddington
The late Pat Brownsdon
Margaret Chadwick
The late Edmund Chaumeton
Willis Cowles
Ted Evans
John Humphreys
Molly Moore

Jack Mound
Jo Peppercorn
Gus Palmer
Violet Simpson
John Stephenson
Nancy Thomas
The late Stanley Tyas
Freddie Walker